# INSTRUCTOR'S MANUAL

to accompany

# CLASSICAL AND OBJECT-ORIENTED SOFTWARE ENGINEERING

Third Edition

## Stephen R. Schach
## Jeffrey G. Gray
*Both of Vanderbilt University*

*IRWIN*

Chicago • Bogotá • Boston • Buenos Aires • Caracas
London • Madrid • Mexico City • Sydney • Toronto

To our families and our students

# CONTENTS

# PREFACE

*Classical and Object-Oriented Software Engineering* can be used as a textbook at two different levels. The material can be used for a junior/senior level course, or for a first year graduate-level course. Not only does the instructor have the freedom to present the lecture material at the appropriate level for the class, but the wide variety of problems allows the instructor to focus the course as desired.

## HOW THIS INSTRUCTOR'S MANUAL IS ORGANIZED

This preface contains teaching suggestions relating to the book as a whole. Each chapter consists of material relating to the corresponding chapter of *Classical and Object-Oriented Software Engineering*, namely teaching suggestions for that specific chapter and solutions to the problems and term project component for that chapter. At the end of this manual are copies of all the figures in *Classical and Object-Oriented Software Engineering* to assist the instructor in preparing transparencies.

## ABOUT THE PROBLEM SETS

There are four different types of problems: exercises, the term project, the case study, and readings in software engineering. All four types have been tested in the classroom. The exercises are of different types, including essay-type problems, numerical problems, and problems that essentially require nothing more than understanding what was taught in class. The instructor may select from the problem sets for each chapter. For example, in Chapter 11, Design Phase, there are two problems using each of the design methods covered in that chapter. If the instructor chooses to cover all the methods in class, then he or she may assign just one of the problems using each method. But if only two design methods are taught, then both the problems using those two methods may be assigned.

In my opinion it is most important that students get experience working in teams developing a software product from beginning to end. In the software industry almost all products are developed by teams, and I believe that we shortchange our students if we do not give them this experience. The size of the team is critical. Three is the smallest team that cannot collaborate over a standard telephone; the term project in the book was designed for teams of that size, and it works well. Of course, few students are considerate enough to ensure that the class size will always be a multiple of three—there will usually have to be one or two teams of size four! The problem with teams of more than three members is that one or two students always seem to end up doing all the work, whereas a team of three usually shares the load evenly among team members.

An important issue is whether to assign students to teams or allow students to choose their own. Fifteen years' experience of teaching software engineering courses has convinced me that students should always choose their own teams. One problem is that not everyone in the class knows everyone else. So I assign different teams for each of the first six components of the term project in such a way that every student has the experience of working with 12 different students. Then the members of the class choose their own teams to work together on the components from Chapter 7 onwards, the point being that the rapid prototype that a team sets up in Chapter 7 is used in the next phase of the term project, whereas the work from Chapters 1 through 6 is not carried forward. The students are warned at the beginning of the course that they will be given a team grade for the term project, and that they should get acquainted with as many class members as possible during the first few weeks. Permanent teams are set up after the first six weeks, so the chances of a team being broken up by a student dropping the class are reduced. Invariably, of course, when I call for the names of team members there are a few students who have not joined a team. These students I assign to their own teams, and these are the teams that come to me with problems of the "we can't get along with one another" variety. Also, the grades of assigned teams seem to be lower than those of the other teams.

A difficulty that sometimes arises within assigned teams is that one team member complains to me that he or she is doing all the work, and that it is unfair that all three team members should get the same grade. In that case, I call a meeting of the team, and ask them to suggest an equitable way of assigning grades. I have always been able to come to an arrangement that is satisfactory to all three members of the team. However, it is not pleasant to have to deal with such issues, and it only reinforces my belief that assigned teams are undesirable.

The case study problems were included because of the belief held by many educators that beginners can learn more from modifying an existing solution than by struggling to create a new solution from scratch. This approach is particularly appropriate to the study of software engineering; after all, most software professionals modify (maintain) existing products, rather than create (develop) new products.

When I teach undergraduate courses, I assign almost all the exercises, and either the term project or case study problems. It would be difficult to expect the class to complete both the term project and the case study problems. I assign case study problems when my colleagues warn me that the class is not quite as good as the previous year's.

The fourth type of problem in the text is based on readings in software engineering. This material is more suitable for graduate students than undergraduates. When teaching graduate students I assign equal weight to the exercises, readings, and term project. Of course, it is unreasonable to assign all the exercises and readings as well as the entire term project, so I select from the exercises and readings.

At the end of the semester, I feel that I have succeeded if the students have learned how to specify, plan, design, implement, maintain, test, and so on, working as a member of a team. The best way I can determine this is to make the course project-oriented. I grade the components of the term project extremely carefully. I experiment with the students' prototypes and implementations, ask walkthrough-style questions about their designs, and so on. Students generally enjoy showing off their work, so I organize sessions at which I examine the work of each team in the presence of their classmates; teams have the option of a private demonstration, but no team has as yet chosen this.

The term project has been designed generically. That is to say, it consists of fourteen components that can be applied to any term project of the instructor's choosing, not just the project in *Classical and Object-Oriented Software Engineering*. The project has been broken up into pieces so that the instructor can soon detect if a team has fallen behind. If this happens, remedial action can quickly be taken to help the team get back on track. Also, asking for fourteen different items to be handed in on fourteen different occasions usually results in documentation of higher quality than if the specifications, design, implementation, and so on are all handed in at the end of the semester. Finally, I find it much easier to grade fourteen small pieces of a term project at my leisure during the semester than one gargantuan project at a time when I have end-of-semester deadlines to meet.

## LECTURE OUTLINES

Returning to the lecture material, I comfortably cover the entire book in one semester, including time for questions and discussion. When teaching undergraduates, I do it as follows:

| | |
|---|---|
| Lecture 1 | Course objectives, introduction to software engineering teams |
| Lectures 2–4 | Chapter 1 |
| Lectures 5–6 | Chapter 2 |
| Lectures 7–8 | Chapter 3 |
| Lectures 9–11 | Chapter 4 |
| Lectures 12–14 | Chapter 5 |
| Lectures 15–17 | Chapter 6 |
| Lectures 18–20 | Chapter 7 |
| Lectures 21–24 | Chapter 8 (excluding 8.8 and 8.9) |
| Lectures 25 | Midterm examination |
| Lectures 26–28 | Chapter 9 |
| Lectures 29–31 | Chapter 10 |
| Lectures 32–35 | Chapter 11 |
| Lectures 36–38 | Chapter 12 |
| Lectures 39–42 | Chapter 13 |
| Lecture 43–44 | Chapter 14 |
| Lecture 45 | Course review and wrap-up |

I also conduct laboratory sessions to introduce the students to UNIX, C++, and workstations. I have found that students quickly pick up everything else that they need to know for the term project from manuals, fellow team members, and other students. By the end of the course they are equipped to work as software engineers.

When teaching first year graduate students I go through the material in 32 lectures, in order to leave time for discussing research papers in software engineering (and specifically in object-oriented software engineering). I cover the material as follows:

| | |
|---|---|
| Chapter 1 | 2 lectures |
| Chapter 2 | 1.5 lectures |
| Chapter 3 | 1.5 lectures |
| Chapter 4 | 2.5 lectures |
| Chapter 5 | 2.5 lectures |
| Chapter 6 | 3 lectures |
| Chapter 7 | 2 lectures |

| Chapter 8 | 2.5 lectures |
|-----------|--------------|
| Chapter 9 | 2 lectures |
| Chapter 10 | 1.5 lectures |
| Chapter 11 | 3 lectures |
| Chapter 12 | 2 lectures |
| Chapter 13 | 4 lectures |
| Chapter 14 | 2 lectures |

Not only can graduate students easily assimilate the course material at this pace, but they enjoy impressing me by doing far more elaborate term projects than their undergraduate counterparts. Also, they are usually familiar with UNIX-based workstations, so they do not need to spend time learning the basics of practical software engineering.

The material can be presented in a number of different ways. Detailed transparencies highlighting the key points of the text can be used. Alternatively, transparencies of the figures can be prepared using the material in this instructor's manual. It does not really matter how *Classical and Object-Oriented Software Engineering* is taught—all that is needed is enthusiasm. May you have as much fun and satisfaction teaching from *Classical and Object-Oriented Software Engineering* as I have had.

Stephen R. Schach

# CHAPTER 1

# SCOPE OF SOFTWARE ENGINEERING

One major theme of this chapter is the importance of maintenance in the software life process. Another is the wide range of areas of knowledge encompassed by software engineering. It would not be a good idea to omit any of the sections of Chapter 1 because the material is used in later chapters.

## PROBLEM SOLUTIONS

1.1: Development constitutes 33% of the total software production budget. The breakdown is then: requirements $29,100, specification $38,750, planning $19,400, design $58,200, module coding and testing $116,350, integration $58,200.

1.2: Try to find a solution using off-the-shelf software (packages). If this fails, determine which of the constraints (time, cost, functionality) can be relaxed, and provide a solution that fits the remaining constraints. If this fails, do not make promises that cannot be kept, but rather provide data such as hardware invoices and software development schedules showing the unreasonableness of the total request. If that does not convince the client of the unreasonableness of his demands, then you do not want him as a client.

1.3: Acceptance criteria must be stipulated in the contract, as must a full list of deliverables. Clauses should include: software must meet specifications, be delivered on time, within budget; all faults must be corrected at no further charge for a period of one year, say, after acceptance of product; documentation must be full and complete, and must include source code, specifications, design, and operating instructions; training must be provided (stipulate type and duration). Terms of the maintenance contract should be included. You might try to include a clause holding the developer responsible for damages caused by faults in the software.

1.4: *Late delivery:* underestimation of size of product; failure to obtain complete and accurate requirements; poor planning; failure to specify the product correctly; poor management techniques; failure to detect faults early in life cycle; ineffective or badly trained personnel; poor quality testing; poor documentation of development process; personnel turnovers; poor communication between members of the development team; continual hardware and/or system software failures.

*Project over budget:* all of the above, plus unexpected price increases for hardware, programming tools, etc.

*Product does not meet specifications:* poor quality specifications; poor testing; poor quality assurance.

*Damage to aircraft:* poor testing, and hence residual faults; bad documentation.

*Inadequate documentation:* poor management.

1.5: Approximately $67. From Figure 1.5, the ratio of cost of detecting and correcting a fault during the maintenance phase to the cost of detecting and correcting it during the specifications phase is approximately 184 to 1.

1.6: Approximately $335. From Figure 1.5, the ratio of cost of detecting and correcting a fault during the maintenance phase to the cost of detecting and correcting it during the implementation phase is approximately 37 to 1.

1.7: Point out that 60% to 70% of all detected faults are specification or design faults and thus the request to find faults early is reasonable.

1.8: A variety of definitions are applicable, including those incorporating concepts like "organized," "unified," or "whole."

1.9: Suggest tactfully that it is unlikely that there is only one "bug." Save the lecture on avoiding the use of the word "bug" until later.

1.10: If the software developers have little experience with the object-oriented paradigm, additional time and money will be needed for proper training. Although future benefits will be realized from training the staff, training may result in this particular project running late and over-budget. Thus, if delivery deadline and cost are critical, then it may make more sense to use the structured paradigm.

However, if the developers have a comfortable understanding of the object-oriented paradigm, then that is what should be utilized. Using the object-oriented paradigm should result in a product that is easier and quicker to develop, has fewer faults, and is easier to maintain.

## TERM PROJECT

1.11: The existing product should have been designed with an architecture that will allow modifications to be made to one component without significantly disrupting other components of the product. All that then needs to be done is to change the code to compute the value of a masterwork to reflect the new formula. This is a relatively simple task, provided that the new method does not require information about masterworks that was not available in the previous version. This is clearly better than starting again from scratch.

# CHAPTER 2

# SOFTWARE PRODUCTION AND ITS DIFFICULTIES

This chapter consists of two parts, both providing an overview of software production and its difficulties, but from two very different viewpoints. Sections 2.1 through 2.9 have been included because few students have any experience at all with the software industry. The material is essentially an expansion of the life-cycle model described in Section 1.3, together with a description of the attendant difficulties.

Section 2.10 constitutes the second part of the chapter. Brooks' *No Silver Bullet* has been described as the most important article on software engineering of the past ten years. Whether or not this is an exaggeration, Brooks' ideas are surely destined to have as great an impact on the software engineering community as his book *The Mythical Man-Month* has had since 1975. In my opinion, his concepts of complexity, conformity, changeability, and invisibility will be frequently referenced in the future, as will his use of Aristotle's categories of essence and accidents.

## PROBLEM SOLUTIONS

2.1: An instructor builds a database for student grades.
The owner of a small business writes his or her own packages for inventory and accounts payable.

2.2: No independent SQA means that there may well be residual faults. Also, the developer may not document the product adequately. This may cause problems during the maintenance phase if the developer's recollection of all details is not adequate.

2.3: Developer fully understands client's requirements. No rapid prototyping is necessary. Also, specifications will be unambiguously understood. In fact, communication problems of all kinds are minimized.

2.4: In general, there is no difference.

2.5: The objectives and activities of the two phases are so different that it makes no sense at all. The requirements phase is a somewhat informal process of determining the client's needs, while the activities of the specification phase consist of drawing up a precise statement of exactly what the product is to do, followed by the drawing up of a detailed plan for doing it.

2.6:     *Requirements phase:* record of discussions with client; document stating client's needs and/or a rapid prototype; record of SQA review.

         *Specification phase:* specification document; record of SQA review.

         *Planning phase:* software project management plan; record of SQA review.

         *Design phase:* architectural design; detailed design of each module; record of SQA review.

         *Implementation phase:* source code; comments in the source code; test cases for each module; record of SQA testing.

         *Integration phase:* commented source code of product as a whole; test cases for product as a whole; user manual, operator manual, other manuals; record of SQA testing.

         *Maintenance phase:* record of changes made, with reasons; regression test cases; modified documentation from previous phases; record of SQA testing.

         *Retirement phase:* why it was retired, when, and by whom.

2.7:     No. Testing must never be a separate phase, but an intrinsic and essential co-activity of all phases.

2.8:     Not reasonable (see Chapter 14 of *Classical and Object-Oriented Software Engineering* for full details). We have to change the attitude towards maintenance in the computer industry, primarily by paying maintainers at least as much money as developers and increasing their status.

2.9:     If a product performs useful work, but is for some reason no longer maintainable, then it is likely that the product will be rewritten so that it can continue to perform useful work, rather than being retired. True retirement takes place only if the perceived need for the product has completely disappeared.

2.10:     Maintenance becomes difficult, because the only way to understand the product as a whole is to read the source code of the entire product. Also, the sole documentation on an individual module is the source code of that module. In addition, lack of documentation means that the chance of a regression fault increases.

2.11:     Refer to Figure 2.1. Complexity of all four is high, but lower than that of software, because there are fundamental principles underlying each that reduce complexity. All except theology have to conform to societal needs. Law has a built-in inertia to change, whereas medicine and engineering have to react to changes in technology and science. However, engineering is bound by physical laws, engineering principles, and engineering codes. Theology does change with societal pressure (e.g., female clergy) but slower than the other three. Engineering alone is visualizable.

2.12:     Answers will clearly depend on the individual, but the usual responses include parallel processing, network operating systems, object-oriented paradigm, C++, 4GLs, and UNIX.

| | Law | Medicine | Theology | Engineering |
|---|---|---|---|---|
| Complexity | high | high | high | high |
| Conformity | high | high | low | high |
| Changeability | low | high | low | intermediate |
| Invisibility | high | high | very high | low |

Figure 2.1. Complexity of other areas of knowledge.

## TERM PROJECT

2.14: *Complexity:* Even a straightforward and relatively small-scale product like that required by Osbert Oglesby exhibits complexity. This complexity will show up in the form of unexpected faults during both development and maintenance.

*Conformity:* It is likely that Osbert Oglesby will insist that certain reports conform in format to similar reports currently used in his business.

*Changeability:* Problem 1.11 is one example of the many enhancements that will probably need to be made in the future. In addition, as the fine arts market changes, Osbert will probably have to modify his purchasing policies to compete successfully.

*Invisibility:* Like all software, the Osbert Oglesby product is not very visible. Visibility may be improved by breaking the product into three largely independent pieces, namely the parts that deal with masterpieces, masterworks, and other.

# CHAPTER 3

# SOFTWARE LIFE-CYCLE MODELS

The central idea of this chapter is the interplay between the waterfall model and the rapid prototyping model. The waterfall model is the "traditional" way of developing software, the rapid prototyping is the "modern" way of doing it. But the waterfall model has certainly not been superseded by the rapid prototyping model. On the contrary, many major software organizations feel that the proven advantages of the waterfall model far outweigh its equally proven disadvantages. My objective in writing this chapter was to enable the student to select an appropriate life-cycle model for a given project.

The spiral model (Section 3.5) is becoming increasingly fashionable. As a result, it is being used in domains for which it is inapplicable (see Section 3.5.1). It is important for the students to know both when and when not to use each life-cycle model.

More and more software organizations of all kinds are showing great interest in the capability maturity model (Section 3.7). For this reason, students should be exposed to the CMM, if only at the overview level. ISO 9000 (Section 3.8) is equally important.

## PROBLEM SOLUTIONS

3.1:   Build-and-fix. There is nothing to be gained by using a more sophisticated model.

3.2:   Experience and skills of the development team; computer literacy of the client; extent to which the client seems to appreciate his or her real needs; whether evolutionary delivery is acceptable.

3.3:   The product may not be what the client really needs, so construct a rapid prototype. The design may not permit future development as the footwear organization grows or changes the way it does business, so ensure that the design is as open-ended as is reasonable. There may be cost and or time overruns, so estimate carefully (see Chapter 10). The users may not be comfortable with the product, so a rapid prototype of the user interface is needed; also, involve the purchasing clerks, factory supervisors, sales clerks, and so on, in the development loop. A competitor may produce off-the-shelf software before the product has been delivered—there is no honest way to resolve this risk. A critical member of the development team may leave, so keep management abreast of major decisions being made, thus making it easier to integrate a replacement into the team. The development team may not be properly managed, so ensure that managers are competent and well-trained.

3.4: There is no need for a rapid prototype here—the existing product is the prototype for the new one. The key aspect now is to achieve portability, maintainability, and generality. Excellent documentation is essential for this, so the waterfall model is a strong candidate.

3.5: A comprehensive management information system that is to be phased in over a number of years.

3.6: Software controlling a nuclear power plant, where everything has to work together from the beginning, or an air traffic control system.

3.7: A flight control system that is developed in-house.

3.8: A small product, or any form of contract software.

3.9: The first and most important step is to ensure that senior management is totally committed to the scheme. Without such a commitment, there is no possible way that you can succeed. You should have obtained this commitment at the time you were hired, preferably in writing.


## TERM PROJECT


3.10: The combination of the waterfall and rapid prototyping models described in Section 3.3.1 of *Classical and Object-Oriented Software Engineering* should be used. Rapid prototyping will let the client and users obtain a good idea of how the finished product will look. The strength of the waterfall model is that it is document driven; documentation is generated at every phase. There is also testing performed by SQA at every phase.

# CHAPTER 4

# STEPWISE REFINEMENT, CASE AND OTHER TOOLS OF THE TRADE

Students love Section 4.1.1, because someone in the class usually discovers the fault in the design before I point it out to them, and I sometimes have a tough time convincing them that the fault is deliberate! The concept of stepwise refinement is used throughout the rest of the book, so it is worthwhile spending a little time ensuring that every member of the class understands the concept.

Other important sections are those introducing cost–benefit analysis (Section 4.2), CASE (Sections 4.3 through 4.8), and software metrics (Section 4.9). All these concepts thoroughly permeate the remainder of the book.

## PROBLEM SOLUTIONS

4.1–4.5: The action to be taken when two successive transaction records have the same key is shown in Figure 4.1.

In the flowchart of Figure 4.2 the assumption has been made that the last record in the old master file is a dummy record with key ZZZZZZ to ensure that the end of the old master file is never encountered before the end of the transaction file. In addition, it is assumed that the transaction file and the old master file are sorted as specified in the text.

| Next Transaction <br> Current Transaction | INSERT | MODIFY | DELETE |
|---|---|---|---|
| INSERT | Error condition | Insert, then modify | Do nothing |
| MODIFY | Impossible if input file is sorted | Perform second modification | Delete record |
| DELETE | Impossible if input file is sorted | Impossible if input file is sorted | Error condition |

Figure 4.1. Action to be taken when two successive transaction records have the same key.

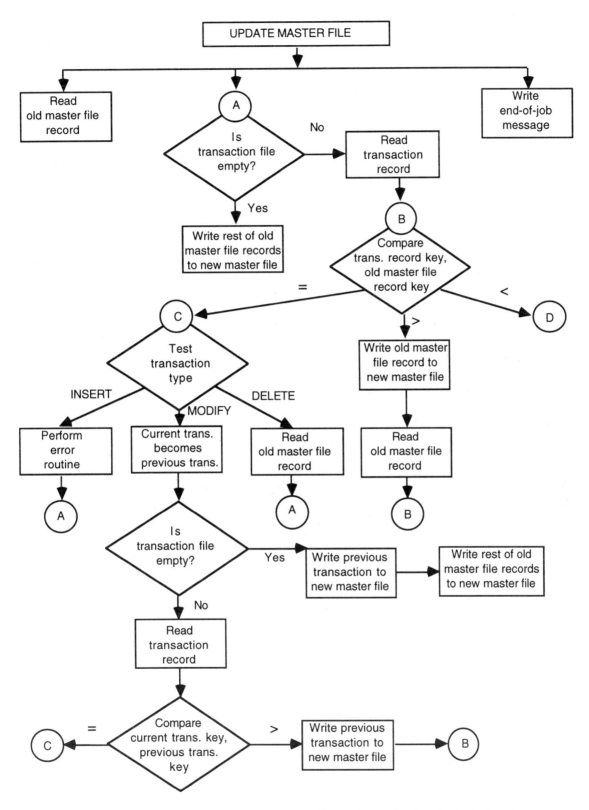

Figure 4.2. Flowchart for sequential file update using level-1 lookahead.

10

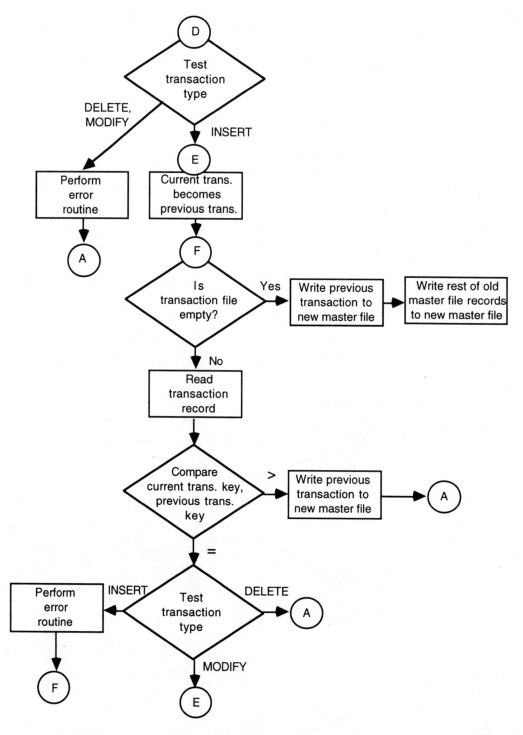

Figure 4.2. Flowchart for sequential file update using level-1 lookahead (continued).

The flowchart of Figure 4.2 provides a solution to all the problems stated.

*4.6:*     *There are six possible orderings:*

1. INSERT, DELETE, MODIFY. This does not work when an INSERT is followed by a DELETE of the same record.
2. INSERT, MODIFY, DELETE. Ordering in the text.
3. DELETE, INSERT, MODIFY. This does not work because INSERT has to precede both DELETE and MODIFY.

4, 5, 6. Same reason as 3; INSERT has to precede both DELETE and MODIFY.

4.7: Cost–benefit analysis will help the committee to decide whether it would be more advantageous for the Velorian government to do nothing, or take active steps to alleviate the problem.

Health care costs are of two types, preventative medicine (inoculating the populace, assuming that a vaccine exists) and treating the victims. The cost of preventative medicine can be estimated by multiplying the total number of Velorians by the cost of inoculation; the latter figure can be furnished by the Department of Health on the basis of previous inoculation campaigns. The cost of future treatment can be estimated using data regarding the cost of treating current victims of the disease; its future incidence can be estimated using epidemiological methods. The total treatment cost is then the cost per victim times the estimated future number of victims.

Loss of earnings and taxes for two weeks' sickness can be estimated from tax records, assuming that the disease attacks members of every socioeconomic group equally.

Pain and discomfort can be estimated by examining the awards for damages in civil suits with a similar level of discomfiture.

Gratitude towards the government could be estimated by multiplying the cost (in government spending) of buying a vote by the number of votes estimated to be lost to the opposition if the disease is not eradicated; the latter figure can be obtained by taking an opinion poll.

4.8–9: A configuration management tool is highly desirable because it is difficult for anyone to keep control over multiple modules, irrespective of the size of the development organization. If a configuration management tool costs too much for a small organization, then just a version control tool will have to suffice; it may come as part of the operating system.

4.10: Ron, Stella, and Ted make local copies of each of the four modules, and determine what changes each will make. Each in turn then freezes the current version of all four modules, makes changes, and has the changes tested by the SQA group. The changed version becomes the baseline version, local copies of which are then distributed to the remaining maintenance programmers. The baseline versions of the four modules must be under the personal control of the manager to ensure that this procedure is followed exactly in the absence of an automated tool.

4.11: A CASE environment implicitly or explicitly incorporates a software process. An organization that has reached level 3 has a fully documented process in place, and a CASE environment can then be used to automate that process. However, introducing a CASE environment to a level 1 or level 2 organization almost invariably has the effect of imposing a process (that may or not be appropriate) onto an organization that is not ready to adopt any software process at all. The result is usually disastrous.

4.12:   Almost any CASE tool that is relevant to the individual tasks being performed will help the organization.  For example, a version control tool could assist in keeping track of the different versions of a source file.

## TERM PROJECT

4.13:   The answer will depend on the level of maturity of the development organization. However, every organization will need configuration control and build tools, such as those described in Sections 4.4 through 4.6 of the text.  In addition, other relevant tools, such as screen and report generators, interactive debuggers, and documentation tools, will prove to be of assistance.

# CHAPTER 5
## TESTING PRINCIPLES

The major theme of this chapter is that testing is not a separate phase of the life cycle, but an activity that is carried on continuously throughout the life cycle, from the beginning to the end.

It is important that two distinctions be carefully drawn. The first is the difference between execution-based and nonexecution-based testing. For many students, the very idea of nonexecution-based testing is difficult to comprehend. The second is the difference between testing and correctness proving. The correctness proof of Section 5.5.1 can be understood even by students without college-level mathematics.

## PROBLEM SOLUTIONS

5.1:   *Correctness proving* is the use of mathematical proof techniques to show that the product satisfies its specifications.

*Verification* is used in two ways, namely (a) nonexecution-based testing, and (b) the process of determining that a specific activity has been completed correctly.

*Validation* is the process of determining whether the product as a whole satisfies its requirements.

5.2:   If the organization is restructured so that 21 professionals, including three or four managers, are concerned solely with SQA, then increased productivity and product quality can be expected. The costs to the company will include reorganization time (two day's labor, say, approximately $55,000) and training time and costs for three or four SQA managers (perhaps $75,000). The total cost of about $130,000 should be recouped in a year even if productivity increases by only 2%.

5.3:   Suppose that product development is done by five professionals including one manager, while SQA is done by the other two professionals including the other manager. Reorganization costs are now about $5500 (that is, one tenth of the costs for Problem 5.2), and training costs for only one manager are about $22,500. Again the total cost should soon be recouped.

5.4:   Assuming that good testing techniques have been used, it is unlikely that there are any further faults.

5.5: Both are review processes performed by teams with the aim of finding faults. In both cases the material is studied by individual team members, and then the material is reviewed by the team as a group.

The major differences are: an inspection is a formal five-step process while a walk-through has two informal steps; previously acquired fault statistics play an important role in the inspection process; there is a formal component of the inspection process for ensuring that all faults noted are later corrected; if more than a certain fraction of the material is changed then it must be submitted for reinspection.

5.6: The results of the experiments cited in Section 5.2.3 show that inspections both detect faults and save money.

5.7: *Utility:* Is it easy to use? How much training is needed for the package to be used effectively? How easy is the documentation to understand? Is the product reasonably priced compared to similar products on the market? Does it have the features we need?

*Reliability:* How frequently does the product crash? What are the results of such a crash, and how easy is it to resume work?

*Robustness:* How does the product react to invalid input data? What happens if the machine is turned off while data is in the course of being entered? What happens if the user bangs on the keyboard in the middle of a computation?

*Performance:* Can the product keep up with our fastest clerks? Can it handle our largest documents? What printers does it support? If it can handle spooling, how many documents can it spool at once? What are its networking capabilities? What is its response time under peak load?

*Correctness:* Does it function correctly? Are the commands correctly described in the user manual? Does it corrupt files in any way?

5.8: *Utility:* Is it easy to use? What types of encryption are supported? Can it transfer data between different types of hardware? Is it economically priced compared to similar products on the market?

*Reliability:* How accurate is the transmission of both large and small files?

*Robustness:* What happens if a single node or a combination of nodes goes down? How tolerant of line noise and spikes on the line is the product?

*Performance:* What speeds of data transfer are supported? How does performance degrade under increased load? Does the product degrade gracefully without loss of reliability? How secure is the network? What is the largest file and the smallest file that may be transferred?

*Correctness:* Does the product transfer files as laid down in the specifications?

5.9: *Utility:* Is it easy to use? What training is needed? Is the training manual easy to follow?

*Reliability:* If aimed correctly, does it strike the target every time? Does it explode in flight?

*Robustness:* What happens if the missile is dropped? How does it function under battle conditions?

*Performance:* How accurate is the missile? Is its explosive power adequate to destroy any ship? Will a near-miss disable a ship, and if so, under what conditions? How much time elapses between the sighting of a target and the missile being launched? Can it cope with evasive action on the part of the target ship?

*Correctness:* Does the product function as laid down in its specifications?

5.10: The program cannot be proved correct, because there is no way of proving the $k = n$ part of the output specification. If that clause is dropped from the output specification, then termination cannot be proved.

5.11: Since loop invariant (5.4) is true, $k \leq n$. To exit from the loop, condition $k \geq n$ must hold. Thus when the loop terminates $k = n$. Substituting this value for $k$ in (5.4) yields output specification (5.3).

5.12: An annotated flowchart is shown in Figure 5.1.

The input specification is $A: n \in \{1, 2, 3, ...\}$. It clearly holds at all points on the flowchart, and is omitted for simplicity. The assertions at $B$ and $C$ follow trivially.

The loop invariant $D: k \leq n$ and $g = 2^k$ holds the first time the loop is entered, because $k = 1$ and $2^1 = 2$. Assume that it holds at $D$ for some $k = k_0$. Then, if $k_0 \geq n$ the loop terminates, and the output condition is satisfied at $H$. If not, then control passes to $E$; as a result of the failed conditional, $k_0 < n$. Also, $g = 2^{k_0}$ by hypothesis.

At $F$, the value of $k_0$ has been increased by 1, and thus $k_0 \leq n$ and $g = 2^{k_0 - 1}$ as indicated on the flowchart. At $G$, $g$ has been multiplied by 2. The assertion at $G$ follows from the fact that $2 \times 2^{k_0 - 1} = 2^{k_0}$.

The assertion at point $G$ is identical to the assertion which, by hypothesis, holds at point $D$. But point $D$ is topologically identical to point $G$. By induction it follows that the loop invariant holds for all values of $k$, $1 \leq k \leq n$.

All that remains is to prove that the loop terminates. Initially the value of $k$ is equal to 0. Each time the loop is iterated the value of $k$ is increased by 1 by the statement $k \leftarrow k + 1$. As a consequence of the loop invariant, $k$ cannot exceed $n$. Eventually $k$ must therefore reach the value $n$, at which time the loop is exited, and the value of $g$ satisfies the output specification.

5.13: A correctness proof is merely a mathematical demonstration that a product satisfies its *specifications*. The specifications may or may not reflect the client's real needs. There is no connection between the client's needs and correctness proving.

5.14: "Correctness proving can be a very effective way to show both the presence and absence of bugs, when used in conjunction with execution-based testing."

16

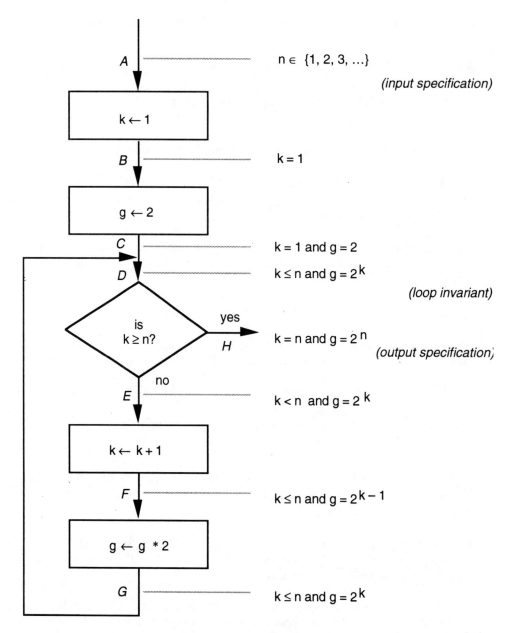

Figure 5.1. Annotated flowchart of code fragment of Problem 5.12.

17

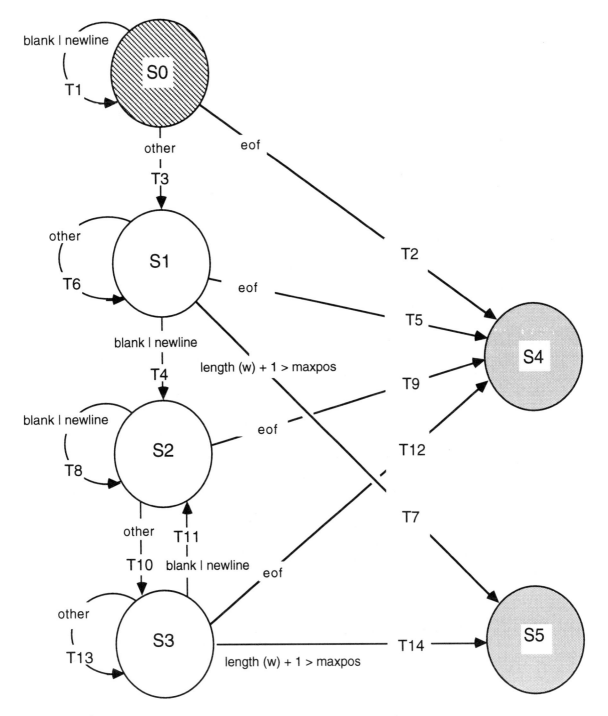

Figure 5.2. Extended FSM for Naur's text processing problem.

5.15: A design using an extended finite state machine (Section 8.6) is given in Figure 5.2.

18

## STATES

S0       <u>Starting state</u>—"Waiting for first character of first word of file"
S1       "Building the first word"
S2       "Waiting for first character of another word"
S3       "Building another word"
S4       <u>Final State</u>—"End-of-file condition"
S5       <u>Final State</u>—"Word longer than MAXPOS characters encountered"

## INPUTS

NEWLINE   New line character
BLANK      Blank character
EOF         End of file condition when read attempted
other        All other characters

## INITIAL CONDITIONS

Variable line_length, integer, number of characters in current output line. Initially 0.
Variable word, character string, word currently being built. Initially empty.
Variable c, current input character. No initial value.
Constant MAXPOS, maximum characters in output line, excluding NEWLINE.

## TRANSITIONS AND ASSOCIATED ACTIONS

T1       Waiting for first word and BLANK or NEWLINE is input
T2       Waiting for first word and EOF is reached
T3       Waiting for first word and other character is input
           word ← c
T4       Building first word and BLANK or NEWLINE is input
           write (word)
           line_length ← length (word)
           word ← null
T5       Building first word and EOF is reached
T6       Building first word and other character is input
           word ← word ∪ c (concatenate word word and character c)
T7       Building first word and its length will be > MAXPOS
T8       Waiting for another word and BLANK or NEWLINE is input
T9       Waiting for another word and EOF is reached
T10      Waiting for another word and other character is input
           word ← word ∪ c
T11      Building another word and BLANK or NEWLINE is input
           **if** line_length + 1 + length (word) > MAXPOS
           {
               write (NEWLINE, word)
               line_length ← length (word)
           }
           **else**
           {
               write (BLANK, word)
               line_length ← line_length + 1 + length (word)
           }
           word ← null

T12      Building another word and EOF reached
                    **if** line_length + 1 + length (word) > MAXPOS
                        write (NEWLINE, word)
                    **else**
                        write (BLANK, word)
T13      Building another word and other character input
                    word ← word ∪ c
T14      Building another word and its length will be > MAXPOS


## C  CODE

```
#include <stdio.h>
#include <string.h>

#define          BLANK              ' '
#define          NEWLINE            '\n'
#define          MAXPOS             10

struct word_type
{
    char              word_arr[80];
    int               length;
} word_type;

FILE *fp;

char get_character (void)
{
    char              character_read;

    character_read = getc (fp);
    if (character_read == EOF)
        return (EOF);
    else if (character_read == NEWLINE)
        return (BLANK);
    else
        return (character_read);
}

void main (void)
{
    char              current_char;       /* current character being processed */
    int               line_length = 0;    /* length of current output  line */
    int               state = 0;          /* current state of finite state machine */
    struct            word_type *word;     /* current word being built */
    char              tmp[1];
    int               i;

    fp = fopen ("data", "r");

    word = (struct word_type *) malloc (sizeof (struct word_type));
    strcpy (word->word_arr, "");          /* initially word is empty */
    word->length = 0;

    while (state < 4)
```

```
                    {
                 current_char = get_character ();
                 switch (state)
                 {
                    case 0:
                    {
                       switch (current_char)
                       {
                          case BLANK:                                    /* T1 */
                             break;

                          case EOF:                                      /* T2 */
                          {
                             state = 4;              /* this terminates loop */
                             break;
                          }

                          default:                                       /* T3 */
                          {
                             word->word_arr[0] = current_char;
                             word->length = 1;
                             state = 1;
                             break;
                          }
                       } /* switch (current_char): case 0 */
                       break;
                    } /* switch (state): case 0 */

                    case 1:
                    {
                       switch (current_char)
                       {
                          case BLANK:                                    /* T4 */
                          {
                             printf ("%s", word->word_arr);
                             strcpy (word->word_arr, "");
                             line_length = word->length;
                             word->length = 0;
                             state = 2;
                             break;
                          }

                          case EOF:                                      /* T5 */
                          {
                             printf ("%s", word->word_arr);
                             state = 4;            /* this terminates loop */
                             break;
                          }

                          default:                                       /* T6 */
                          {
                             if (word->length + 1 > MAXPOS)              /* T7 */
                                state = 5;          /* this terminates loop */
                             else
                             {
                                tmp[0] = current_char;
```

```
                    strncat (word->word_arr, tmp, 1);
                }
                break;
        }
    } /* switch (current_char): case 1 */
    break;
} /* switch (state): case 1 */

case 2:
{
    switch (current_char)
    {
        case BLANK :                                    /* T8 */
            break;

        case EOF:                                       /* T9 */
        {
            state = 4;              /* this terminates loop */
            break;
        }

        default:                                        /* T10 */
        {
            tmp[0] = current_char;
            strncat (word->word_arr, tmp, 1);
            state = 3;
            break;
        }
    } /* switch (current_char): case 2 */
    break;
} /* switch (state): case 2 */

case 3:
{
    switch (current_char)
    {
        case BLANK:                                     /* T11 */
        {
            if ((line_length + 1 + word->length) > MAXPOS)
            {
                printf ("\n");
                printf ("%s", word->word_arr);
                line_length = word->length;
            }
            else
            {
                printf ("%c", BLANK);
                printf ("%s", word->word_arr);
                strcpy (word->word_arr, "");
                line_length = line_length + 1 + word->length;
            }
            word->length = 0;
            state = 2;
            break;
        }
```

22

```
        case EOF:                                              /* T12 */
        {
            if ((line_length + 1 + word->length) > MAXPOS)
            {
                printf ("\n");
                printf ("%s", word->word_arr);
                line_length = word->length;
            }
            else
            {
                printf ("%c", BLANK);
                printf ("%s", word->word_arr);
                line_length = line_length + 1 + word->length;
            }
            state = 4;                  /* this terminates loop */
            break;
        }

        default:                                               /* T13 */
        {
            if ((word->length + 1) > MAXPOS)                   /* T14 */
                state = 5;              /* this terminates loop */
            else
            {
                tmp[0] = current_char;
                strncat (word->word_arr, tmp, 1);
            }
            break;
        }
        } /* switch (current_char): case 3 */
        break;
    } /* switch (state): case 3 */

        default:
            break;
    }  /* switch (state): default */
    }  /* while (state < 4) */

    printf ("\n");
    if (state == 5)
        printf ("Word longer than permitted length encountered\n");

    free (word);
}  /* main */
```

A flowchart for the product is given in Figure 5.3.

23

function get_character:

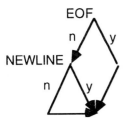

function main:

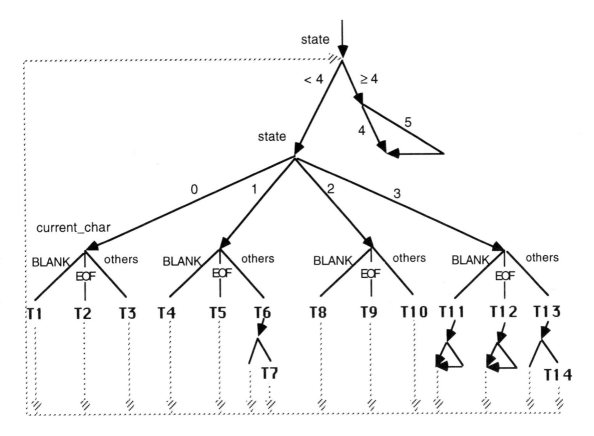

Figure 5.3.  Flowchart of C++ implementation of Naur's text processing problem.

## TERM PROJECT

5.16:  *Utility:* The product should be handed over to the user who can use it and determine if the product is easy to use and whether it performs useful functions. The product will probably not be used if it is not user friendly.

*Reliability:* The product should be run with different sets of data. When there is a failure, the effects of that failure and the time and effort needed to recover from that failure are to be recorded.

*Robustness:* The product should be run with input that violates the input specifications (for example, an integer where a string is expected) to determine if the product fails, or if it can handle the data. It is also necessary to check to see if a valid user command produces undesirable results.

*Performance:* Space should not be a problem. However, timing studies must be performed to determine how much time the program takes to compute various quantities and generate reports.

*Correctness:* Correctness can be tested by performing inspections and also by running test cases for which the output is known and then checking if the output matches the expected results.

Strictly speaking, the only way to determine correctness is to prove the product correct. In practice, performing inspections (nonexecution-based testing) and running black- and glass-box test cases (execution-based testing) can at best give an indication of the correctness of the product.

# CHAPTER 6

# INTRODUCTION TO OBJECTS

The basic message of this chapter is that there is a smooth progression from modules to abstract data types, and finally to objects. There is nothing new or special about objects, notwithstanding the near hysteria surrounding objects both in industry and academia.

## PROBLEM SOLUTIONS

6.1: *Pascal:* procedure or function; both definitions.
*C++:* included file; second definition only.
*Ada:* package or generic; second definition only.

6.2: Coincidental cohesion.
Functional cohesion.
Procedural cohesion.
Functional cohesion.
Procedural cohesion.

6.3: Ensure that modules have high cohesion, and low coupling with other modules. Also, information hiding techniques are important for module reusability. Use of the object-oriented paradigm also promotes reusability.

6.4: Using cost–benefit analysis, decide whether to attempt to reuse only those existing modules that have high cohesion and low coupling, or whether to redesign and recode the modules with unacceptable cohesion and coupling. In all probability, the cost-effective way to proceed will be to discard all but those existing modules with high cohesion and low coupling. Then, determine the cost effectiveness of testing and documenting those modules. Finally, it is essential to ensure that all future modules will be reusable. One way to achieve this is by using the object-oriented paradigm.

6.5: The higher the cohesion of module m, the lower the chance that a change made to m will also have to be made, consistently, to other modules.

6.6: The lower the coupling between module m and other modules, the smaller the chance of inducing a regression fault during maintenance, since m is "independent" of the other modules. Also, low coupling means that details as to how m is implemented are not used by other modules, thereby simplifying maintenance.

6.7: *Data encapsulation:* data structure and the operations performed on it.

*Abstract data type:* data type and the operations performed on instantiations of that type.

6.8:  Abstraction entails thinking about what is done, not how it is done. Information hiding is deliberately hiding as many details as possible from the user. Abstraction is an instance of information hiding.

6.9:  Polymorphism refers to the ability of a function to be applied to different argument types, or an object to refer to instances of various classes at run-time. Dynamic binding selects (from among possible alternatives) the proper version to be chosen at run-time. For example, dynamic binding is used to choose, at run-time, which operation to apply to a polymorphic object. That is to say, at run-time, dynamic binding resolves the various choices that polymorphism offers.

6.10:  Here is a typical solution to the problem:

```
//
// A job queue (of an operating system) is implemented as a two-way linked list.
// New items are added to the rear of the queue and old items are removed from the
// front of the queue.
//

#include <stdio.h>
#include <string.h>
#include <stdlib.h>
#include <iostream.h>


typedef struct  job_record
{
    int                 job_no;
    struct job_record   *in_front;          // points to next record
    struct job_record   *in_rear;           // points to previous record
};

struct job_record          *front_of_queue, *rear_of_queue;
                            // pointers to first and last records in the two-way linked list

void initialize_job_queue (void)
//
// initialize front and rear pointers of queue
//
{
    front_of_queue = NULL;
    rear_of_queue = NULL;

} /* initialize_job_queue */

void add_job_to_queue (int job_number)
//
// add job to queue
//
{
    struct  job_record      *temp;

    temp = (struct job_record *) malloc (sizeof (struct job_record));
```

```
            temp->job_no = job_number;
            temp->in_front = rear_of_queue;
            temp->in_rear = NULL;

            if (front_of_queue == NULL)
                front_of_queue = temp;
            else
                rear_of_queue->in_rear = temp;
            rear_of_queue = temp;

}  // add_job_to_queue

void remove_job_from_queue (int& job_number)
//
// remove first item in queue
//
{
            if (front_of_queue == NULL)
                job_number = -1;
            else
            {
                job_number = front_of_queue->job_no;
                front_of_queue = front_of_queue->in_rear;

                if (front_of_queue = NULL)
                    rear_of_queue = NULL;
                else
                    front_of_queue->in_front = NULL;
            }

}  // remove_job_from_queue

void print_job_queue (void)
//
// print items in job queue
//
{
            struct job_record   *temp;

            temp = front_of_queue;

            cout << endl << "The queue contains:" << endl;

            while (temp != NULL)
            {
                cout << temp->job_no << endl;
                temp = temp->in_rear;
            }

}  // print_job_queue

void main (void)
{
            int                 j;
```

28

```
        initialize_job_queue ();

        cout << endl << "Enter Job Number (non-positive to quit): ";
        cin >> j;

        while (j>0)
        {
            add_job_to_queue (j);
            cout << endl << "Entered: " << j << endl;
            cout << endl << "Enter Job Number (non-positive to quit): ";
            cin >> j;
        }

        print_job_queue ();
        cout << endl << "Will pop top of queue..." << endl;
        remove_job_from_queue (j);
        print_job_queue ();

    } // main
```

6.11: This is not true. Information hiding can be achieved via **private** access.

6.12: The higher the cohesion of module m, the greater the reusability of module m, because if m has high cohesion, this means that the whole of m can be reused.

6.13: The lower the coupling between module m and other modules, the greater the reusability of module m, because the lower the coupling, the greater the chance that m can be reused without having to reuse other modules as well.

6.14: Human beings are resistant to all forms of change, especially shifts in technology. For example, the technology used in compact disc players had existed for several years before it began to be recognized as a standard in the late 1980s. The same could be said of VCRs.

6.17: Ensure that modules have functional or informational cohesion, and data coupling; use object-oriented techniques; code the product in a popular high-level language; document modules meticulously; user interface should be able to handle any similar sort of dialog; isolate the input and output components in separate modules; design the product in such a way that it can be understood by an accountant.

6.18: Ensure that modules have functional or informational cohesion, and data coupling; use object-oriented techniques; product must be designed using levels of abstraction, with hardware dependence restricted to the lowest level modules and carefully documented; code the product in a popular high-level language; document modules meticulously; the modules for searching and updating the catalogue should be written generically; the routines for reading bar-codes routines should be able to handle any standard bar-code; the query-handling component should use standard techniques such as menus that can be reused in other products.

6.19: Retain only those modules which have high cohesion and low coupling with other modules, as well as detailed documentation that has been meticulously updated. Describe the function of each module in a single phrase; use these phrases to set up a KWIC index to the modules. For each module, prepare a one-paragraph description that will enable the user to determine whether or not that module is appropriate for a given product. Prepare detailed documentation on that module for reuse purposes. All this information must be available online. Finally, set up procedures so that software developers have to scan the file of modules before trying to reinvent the wheel.


## TERM PROJECT

6.20: In theory, every part of the product could be reused in future price estimation products for other art dealers. (To maintain his competitive edge, Osbert should ensure that his contract with the software developer explicitly prevents this. The easiest way is for the contract to stipulate that Osbert owns the copyright of the program, thereby preventing any reuse without his permission.)

In addition, modules that carry out common operations, such as updating a file or comparing dates, will be reusable in a wide variety of products.

# CHAPTER 7

# REQUIREMENTS PHASE

In many cases, there are a number of different techniques that can be used in a given project. The results of experiments can be extremely helpful in selecting between them. In Section 7.7 an important experiment is described. But in addition, possible weaknesses of the experiment are pointed out, and the student is warned not to treat the results as "proven facts." All through the rest of the book the same issue is raised: On the one hand, experiments are a vital source of information, while on the other hand, the result of an experiment must be questioned if the experimental technique is flawed. This approach to experimentation is followed throughout the book.

## PROBLEM SOLUTIONS

7.1:    Key points to make include: The fact that the waterfall model has been used "usually with some success" does not necessarily mean that the client's real needs are always met. Customer satisfaction should be the driving force behind all software development, and this can be enhanced by using the rapid prototyping model. Also, the rapid prototyping model reduces the feedback loops characteristic of the waterfall model, thus reducing the time, and hence the cost, to develop the software. At the same time, not much hard-and-fast data is available on rapid prototyping, and there are indications that the model has some drawbacks of its own, especially at the managerial level. Even so, advantages seem to outweigh disadvantages.

7.2:    Typical responses might include: Set up a committee to investigate. Cost of retraining all our personnel is too high. We've been using the waterfall model for years, our bottom line is healthy, and we see no reason to change. The model should be tried on a small project, to enable us to evaluate the rapid prototyping model within our corporate context.

7.3:    In general, interpreted languages are to be preferred over compiled languages.

7.4:    When there is an existing product which exhibits virtually all the desired functionality, then rapid prototyping is unnecessary. For example, if a product has been modified so often that any further changes are likely to induce regression faults, then that product has to be rewritten from scratch before additional maintenance can be performed. Constructing a rapid prototype will not help the developers in any way.

7.5: If the client has an existing product, either manual or automated, with a somewhat similar user interface, then the client can simply indicate the changes that have to be made to the existing user interface.

7.6: Those portions of the rapid prototype that are computer-generated may be reused, as well as portions that are of sufficiently high quality to pass inspection by the SQA group. This latter case is unlikely when "classical" rapid prototyping is employed.

7.7: Development of the product takes longer than necessary.

7.8: The usual reason that we construct a rapid prototype is to determine the client's real needs. The specific paradigm to be followed thereafter, whether structured or object-oriented, is usually irrelevant once that has been done. In addition, research has indicated that rapid prototyping is important within the object-oriented context.


## TERM PROJECT

7.9:
```c
#include <stdio.h>
#include <string.h>
#include <stdlib.h>

/*
 * this is a rapid prototype of the Osbert Oglesby product
 */

#define     NUM_GALLERY_RECORDS    10
#define     NUM_AUCTION_RECORDS    7

#define     TARGET_MARKUP          2.15
#define     ANNUAL_INTEREST        1.085

#define     FALSE                  0
#define     TRUE                   1

struct painting_type
{
    char          first_name[22];
    char          last_name[22];
    char          title[42];
    char          painting_date[9];
    float         height;
    float         width;
    char          medium[11];
    char          subject[11];
};

struct auction_type
{
    painting_type description;
    char          auction_date[9];
    float         sale_price;
};
```

32

```c
struct gallery_type
{
    char            classification[12];
    painting_type   description;
    char            purchase_date[9];
    char            seller_name[21];
    char            seller_addr[26];
    float           alg_price;
    float           purch_price;
    float           target_price;
    char            sale_date[9];
    char            buyer_name[21];
    char            buyer_addr[26];
    float           sell_price;
};

/*
 * global variables
 */


int             gallery_count;
char            current_date[9];
float           fash;
/*
 * because this is a rapid prototype, an array of records has been used to keep
 * track of a number of auction records and gallery records
 */
gallery_type            gallery_records[NUM_GALLERY_RECORDS];
auction_type            auction_records[NUM_AUCTION_RECORDS] =
{
    {"Leonardo", "da Vinci", "Ceiling Painting", "1530", 482.5, 530.9, "oil",
        "other", "11/20/70", 43.4},
    {"Rembrandt", "van Rijn", "The Day Watch", "1650", 90.7, 41.3, "oil",
        "still life", "03/16/63", 13.6},
    {"Frans", "Hals", "The Manic-Depressive Cavalier", "1616", 103.3, 61.7, "oil",
        "portrait", "04/22/86", 23.4},
    {"Edouard", "Manet", "Portrait of Claude Monet", "1871", 43.6, 51.4, "watercolor",
        "portrait", "01/04/52", 1.1},
    {"Claude", "Monet", "Portrait of Edouard Manet", "1871", 43.6, 51.4, "watercolor",
        "portrait", "01/04/52", 1.1},
    {"van Gogh", "Vintcent", "Irises, sunflowers, wheat, and stuff", "1888", 174.2, 89.9, "oil",
        "landscape", "10/31/84", 6.1},
    {"Georges", "Seurat", "Lots of Tiny Colored Dots", "1889", 206.1, 307.6, "oil",
        "landscape", "05/29/90", 20.4},
};

/*------------------------------------------------------------------------------------------------*/

void clear_screen (void)
/*
 * clears the screen
 */
{
    int             i;

    /*
```

```
     * implementation-dependent code to clear screen should replace
     * code given below
     */

    for (i = 0; i < 26; i++)
        printf ("\n");
} /* clear_screen */
```

/*------------------------------------------------------------------------------------*/

```
void press_enter (void)
/*
 * wait until user presses <ENTER> key
 */
{
    char            ch;

    fflush (stdin);
    ch = getchar ();
} /* press_enter */
```

/*------------------------------------------------------------------------------------*/

```
void initialize (void)
/*
 * initializes gallery records
 */
{
    int             count;

    gallery_count = 0;
    fash = 0.5;

    for (count = 0; count < NUM_GALLERY_RECORDS; count++)
        gallery_records[count].sell_price = -1.0;
} /* initialize */
```

/*------------------------------------------------------------------------------------*/

```
int date_compare (char *date1, char *date2)
/*
 * determines temporal order of two dates
 * returns -1 if date1 < date2
 * returns 0 if date1 = date2
 * returns 1 if date2 < date1
 */
{
    int             year1, year2;
    int             month1, month2;
    int             day1, day2;
    char            temp[2];

    temp[0] = date1[6];
    temp[1] = date1[7];
    year1 = atoi (temp);
    temp[0] = date2[6];
```

```
        temp[1] = date2[7];
        year2 = atoi (temp);

        temp[0] = date1[3];
        temp[1] = date1[4];
        day1 = atoi (temp);
        temp[0] = date2[3];
        temp[1] = date2[4];
        day2 = atoi (temp);

        temp[0] = date1[0];
        temp[1] = date1[1];
        month1 = atoi (temp);
        temp[0] = date2[0];
        temp[1] = date2[1];
        month2 = atoi (temp);

        if (year1 < year2)
            return -1;

        if (year1 > year2)
            return 1;

        if (month1 < month2)
            return -1;

        if (month1 > month2)
            return 1;

        if (day1 < day2)
            return -1;

        if (day1 > day2)
            return 1;
        else
            return 0;
} /* date_compare */

/*-------------------------------------------------------------------------------------------*/

void get_description (painting_type &description)
/*
 * retrieves painting description information
 */
{
    clear_screen ();
    printf ("Please enter the following information about the painting:\n");

    fflush (stdin);
    printf ("\n\n");

    printf ("Enter the FIRST name of the artist: ");
    gets (description.first_name);

    printf ("Enter the LAST name of the artist: ");
    gets (description.last_name);
```

```
        printf ("Enter the TITLE of the painting: ");
        gets (description.title);

        printf ("Enter the DATE the painting was created (yyyy): ");
        gets (description.painting_date);

        printf ("Enter the HEIGHT of the painting: ");
        scanf ("%f", &description.height);

        printf ("Enter the WIDTH of the painting: ");
        scanf ("%f", &description.width);
        fflush (stdin);

        printf ("Enter the MEDIUM of the painting: ");
        gets (description.medium);

        printf ("Enter the SUBJECT of the painting: ");
        gets (description.subject);
} /* get_description */

/*---------------------------------------------------------------------------------------------*/

void get_purchase_information (gallery_type &gallery_rec)
/*
 * retrieves additional painting information for gallery record
 */
{
        fflush (stdin);
        printf ("\n\n");

        strcpy (gallery_rec.purchase_date, current_date);

        printf ("Enter the NAME of the seller: ");
        gets (gallery_rec.seller_name);

        printf ("Enter the ADDRESS of the seller: ");
        gets (gallery_rec.seller_addr);

        printf ("Enter the purchase PRICE of the painting: ");
        scanf ("%f", &gallery_rec.purch_price);

        gallery_rec.target_price = gallery_rec.purch_price * TARGET_MARKUP;

} /* get_purchase_information */

/*---------------------------------------------------------------------------------------------*/

void insert_record (gallery_type &the_record)
/*
 * inserts gallery record into proper place
 */
{
        int             i;
        int             temp_count;
        int             found;

        gallery_type temp[NUM_GALLERY_RECORDS];
```

```
        temp_count = 0;
        found = FALSE;

        for (i = 0; i < gallery_count; i++)
        {
            if ((strcmp (the_record.classification, gallery_records[i].classification) <= 0) &&
                        (date_compare (the_record.purchase_date,
                                        gallery_records[i].purchase_date) <= 0) && !found)
            {
                temp[temp_count++] = the_record;
                temp[temp_count++] = gallery_records[i];
                found = TRUE;
            }
            else
                temp[temp_count++] = gallery_records[i];
        }

        if (!found)
            temp[temp_count++] = the_record;
        gallery_count++;

        for (i = 0; i < gallery_count; i++)
            gallery_records[i] = temp[i];
    } /* insert_record */

/*-------------------------------------------------------------------------------------------------*/

    void add_new_rec (gallery_type &gallery_rec)
    /*
     * determines if there is enough space to store new gallery record
     */
    {
        if (gallery_count < NUM_GALLERY_RECORDS)
            insert_record (gallery_rec);
        else
        {
            printf ("Storage for the static array has been exhausted.\n");
            printf ("The record could not be inserted.\n");
            printf ("\n\n");
            printf (" Press <ENTER> to return to main menu...");
            press_enter ();

        }
    } /* add_new_rec */

/*-------------------------------------------------------------------------------------------------*/

    float determine_price (gallery_type &gallery_rec)
    /*
     * determines maximum price to be offered for masterpiece
     */
    {
        float           high;
        float           alg_high;
        float           temp;
        float           auction_area;
```

```
float              gallery_area;
int                i;
int                index;
int                found;
char               auction_date[3];
char               curr_date[3];

high = 0.0;
index = 0;
found = FALSE;

for (i = 0; i < NUM_AUCTION_RECORDS; i++)
{
    temp = 0.0;
    if  ((strcmp (auction_records[i].description.first_name,
                  gallery_rec.description.first_name) == 0) &&
         (strcmp (auction_records[i].description.last_name,
                  gallery_rec.description.last_name) == 0))
    {
        if (strcmp (auction_records[i].description.medium,
                    gallery_rec.description.medium) == 0)
            temp++;
        if (strcmp (auction_records[i].description.subject,
                    gallery_rec.description.subject) == 0)
            temp++;

        auction_area = (auction_records[i].description.height) *
                       (auction_records[i].description.width);
        gallery_area = (gallery_rec.description.height) *
                       (gallery_rec.description.width);

        if (auction_area > gallery_area)
            temp = temp * gallery_area / auction_area;
        else
            temp = temp * auction_area / gallery_area;

        if (temp > high)
        {
            high = temp;
            index = i;
            found = TRUE;

        }
    }
}

for (i = 0; i < 3; i++)
{
    auction_date[i] = auction_records[index].auction_date[6+i];
    curr_date[i] = current_date[6+i];
}

alg_high = 0.0;

if (found)
    alg_high = auction_records[index].sale_price;
```

38

```c
      for (i = atoi (auction_date); i < atoi (curr_date); i++)
          alg_high = alg_high * ANNUAL_INTEREST;
      return alg_high;
} /* determine_price */

/*-------------------------------------------------------------------------------------------*/

void buy_masterpiece (void)
/*
 * allows user to buy masterpiece
 */
{
    char            ch;
    gallery_type    temp_painting;

    strcpy (temp_painting.classification, "Masterpiece");

    get_description (temp_painting.description);
    temp_painting.alg_price = determine_price (temp_painting);
    if (temp_painting.alg_price > 0)
    {
        printf ("\nThe algorithm determines the maximum price for this painting to be:\n");
        printf ("$ %-6.2f %s", temp_painting.alg_price, " million dollars.\n\n");

        printf ("Do you want to purchase this painting (Y/N)? ");
        fflush (stdin);
        ch = getchar ();

        if ((ch == 'Y') || (ch == 'y'))
        {
            get_purchase_information (temp_painting);
            add_new_rec (temp_painting);
        }
    }
    else
        printf ("\nThe algorithm has suggested that you should not buy this painting.");

    printf ("\n\n");
    printf ("  Press <ENTER> to return to main menu...");
    press_enter ();
} /* buy_masterpiece */

/*-------------------------------------------------------------------------------------------*/

void buy_masterwork (void)
/*
 * allows user to buy masterwork
 */
{
    clear_screen ();

    printf ("This option is not implemented in the prototype.");

    printf ("\n\n");
    printf ("  Press <ENTER> to return to main menu...");
    press_enter ();
} /* buy_masterwork */
```

```
/*------------------------------------------------------------------------------------*/

void buy_other (void)
/*
 * allows user to buy "other" type of painting
 */
{
    char            ch;
    gallery_type    temp_painting;

    strcpy (temp_painting.classification, "Other");

    get_description (temp_painting.description);

    temp_painting.alg_price =   fash * (temp_painting.description.height) *
                                (temp_painting.description.width);

    if (temp_painting.alg_price > 0)
    {
        printf ("\nThe algorithm determines the maximum price for this painting to be:\n");
        printf ("$ %-6.2f %s", temp_painting.alg_price, " million dollars.\n\n");

        printf ("Do you want to purchase this painting (Y/N)? ");
        fflush (stdin);
        ch = getchar ();

        if ((ch == 'Y') || (ch == 'y'))
        {
            get_purchase_information (temp_painting);
            add_new_rec (temp_painting);
        }
    }
    else
        printf ("\nThe algorithm has suggested that you should not buy this painting.");

    printf ("\n\n");
    printf ("  Press <ENTER> to return to main menu...");
    press_enter ();
} /* buy_other */

/*------------------------------------------------------------------------------------*/

void update_fash (void)
/*
 * allows user to update constant fashionability coefficient
 */
{
    clear_screen ();
    printf ("This prototype uses a single fashionability coefficient for all artists.\n");
    printf ("The final implementation must maintain coefficients for each artist.\n\n");
    printf ("The current value of the fashionability coefficient is: ");
    printf ("%f\n\n", fash);
    printf ("Please enter the new value for the coefficient: ");
    scanf ("%f", &fash);

    printf ("\n\n");
```

```
        printf (" Press <ENTER> to return to main menu...");
        press_enter ();
} /* update_fash */

/*-------------------------------------------------------------------------------------------*/

void buy_painting (void)
/*
 * allows user to select type of painting to be purchased
 */
{

    int             done;
    int             choice;

    done = FALSE;
    while (!done)
    {
        clear_screen ();
        printf ("                   BUY PAINTING MENU\n\n\n");
        printf ("        Osbert Oglesby - Collector of Fine Art\n\n\n");
        printf ("\t        1. Buy a Masterpiece\n\n");
        printf ("\t        2. Buy a Masterwork\n\n");
        printf ("\t        3. Buy an Other piece of work\n\n");
        printf ("\t        4. Update Fashionability Coefficient\n\n");
        printf ("\t        5. Return to Main Menu\n\n\n");
        printf ("        Enter your choice and press <ENTER>: ");
        scanf ("%d", &choice);

        switch (choice)
        {
            case 1:
                buy_masterpiece ();
                break;

            case 2:
                buy_masterwork ();
                break;

            case 3:
                buy_other ();
                break;

            case 4:
                update_fash ();
                break;

            case 5:
                done = TRUE;
                break;

            default:
                printf ("\n\nChoice is out of range\n\n");
                printf ("    Press <ENTER> to return to menu...");
                press_enter ();
                break;
        }
```

```
    }
} /* buy_painting */

/*--------------------------------------------------------------------------------------------*/

void sell_painting (void)
/*
 * allows user to sell a painting in the gallery
 */
{
    int                 i;
    int                 found;
    char                first_name[21];
    char                last_name[21];
    char                title[41];

    fflush (stdin);
    clear_screen ();

    printf ("\n\nPlease enter the following information describing the painting:\n\n");

    printf ("Enter the FIRST name of the artist: ");
    gets (first_name);

    printf ("Enter the LAST name of the artist: ");
    gets (last_name);

    printf ("Enter the TITLE of the painting: ");
    gets (title);

    found = FALSE;

    for (i = 0; i < NUM_GALLERY_RECORDS; i++)
    {
        if  ((strcmp (gallery_records[i].description.first_name, first_name) == 0) &&
             (strcmp (gallery_records[i].description.last_name, last_name) == 0) &&
             (strcmp (gallery_records[i].description.title, title) == 0))
        {
            found = TRUE;
            break;
        }
    }

    if (gallery_records[i].sell_price > 0)
        printf ("\n\nThe painting you described has already been sold!\n\n");
    else
    {
        if (found == TRUE)
        {
            printf ("\n\nPlease enter the following sale information: \n\n\n");

            strcpy (gallery_records[i].sale_date, current_date);

            printf ("Enter the NAME of the buyer: ");
            gets (gallery_records[i].buyer_name);

            printf ("Enter the ADDRESS of the buyer: ");
```

42

```
                    gets (gallery_records[i].buyer_addr);

                    printf ("Enter the selling PRICE: ");
                    scanf ("%f", &gallery_records[i].sell_price);

                    printf ("\n\nThe sale has been recorded.");
                }
            else
                {
                    printf ("\n\nThe painting you described can not be found in the gallery.\n");
                    printf ("Please make sure you entered the above information correctly.\n");
                    printf ("Proper case is required.\n");
                }
        }

    printf ("\n\n");
    printf (" Press <ENTER> to return to main menu...");
    press_enter ();
} /* sell_painting */

/*------------------------------------------------------------------------------------------*/

void bought_report (void)
/*
 * displays report of paintings bought
 */
{
    int                 i;
    float               total_purchase;
    float               total_max;

    total_purchase = 0.0;
    total_max = 0.0;

    clear_screen ();

    for (i = 0; i < gallery_count; i++)
        {
            if ((( i % 3) == 0) && (i != 0))
                {
                    printf ("\n\n");
                    printf (" Press <ENTER> to view the next screen...");
                    press_enter ();
                }

            if ((i % 3) == 0)
                {
                    clear_screen ();
                    printf ("\n\n");
                    printf ("                              REPORT\n");
                    printf ("                 Osbert Oglesby - Collector of Fine Art\n");
                    printf ("                         BOUGHT PAINTINGS\n\n");
                }

                printf ("----------------------------------------------------------------\n");
                printf ("CLASSIFICATION: ");
```

```
        if (gallery_records[i].purch_price > gallery_records[i].alg_price)
            printf ("*");

        printf ("%s %s", gallery_records[i].classification, "  ");
        printf ("\t%s %s\n", "PURCHASE DATE: ", gallery_records[i].purchase_date);
        printf ("%s %s", "LAST NAME:     ", gallery_records[i].description.last_name);
        printf ("\t\t%s %s\n", "TITLE:        ", gallery_records[i].description.title);
        printf ("%s %-0.2f", "SUGG. PRICE:  ", gallery_records[i].alg_price);
        printf ("\t\t%s %-0.2f\n", "PURCHASE PRICE:", gallery_records[i].purch_price);

        total_purchase = total_purchase + gallery_records[i].purch_price;
        total_max = total_max + gallery_records[i].alg_price;
    }

    if (total_max > 0)
        printf ("%s %-0.2f", "\n\nAverage ratio: ", total_purchase / total_max);
    else
        printf ("There are no paintings in the gallery.");

    printf ("\n\n");
    printf ("  Press <ENTER> to return to main menu...");
    press_enter ();
} /* bought_report */

/*----------------------------------------------------------------------------------------*/

void report (void)
/*
 * allows user to select type of report to be displayed
 */
{
    int             done;
    int             choice;

    done = FALSE;
    while (!done)
    {
        clear_screen ();
        printf ("                    REPORT MENU\n\n\n");
        printf ("            Osbert Oglesby - Collector of Fine Art\n\n\n");
        printf ("            1. Report on Bought Paintings\n\n");
        printf ("            2. Report on Sold Paintings\n\n");
        printf ("            3. Report on Fashion Trends\n\n");
        printf ("            4. Return to Main Menu\n\n\n");
        printf ("        Enter your choice and press <ENTER>: ");
        scanf ("%d", &choice);

        switch (choice)
        {
            case 1:
                bought_report ();
                break;

            case 2:
                clear_screen ();
                printf ("\t\t        REPORT ON SOLD PAINTINGS\n\n");
                printf ("\t\t   This report is not implemented in the prototype\n\n\n");
```

```
                    printf ("     Press <ENTER> to return to the menu...");
                    press_enter ();
                    break;

            case 3:
                    clear_screen ();
                    printf ("\t\t            REPORT ON CURRENT FASHIONS\n\n");
                    printf ("\t\t    This report is not implemented in the prototype\n\n\n");

                    printf ("     Press <ENTER> to return to the menu...");
                    press_enter ();
                    break;

            case 4:
                    done = TRUE;
                    break;

            default:
                    printf ("\n\nChoice is out of range\n\n");
                    printf ("     Press <ENTER> to return to menu...");
                    press_enter ();
                    break;
        }
    }
} /* report */

/*-------------------------------------------------------------------------------------------------*/

void main_menu (void)
/*
 * displays main menu containing all the options available to user
 */
{

    int             done;
    int             choice;

    done = FALSE;
    while (!done)
    {

        clear_screen ();
        printf ("\t                MAIN MENU\n\n\n");
        printf ("\t     Osbert Oglesby - Collector of Fine Art\n\n\n");
        printf ("\t         1. Buy a Painting\n\n");
        printf ("\t         2. Sell a Painting\n\n");
        printf ("\t         3. Produce a Report\n\n");
        printf ("\t         4. Quit \n\n\n");
        printf ("\t     Enter your choice and press <ENTER>: ");
        scanf ("%d", &choice);

        switch (choice)
        {
            case 1:
                    buy_painting ();
                    break;
```

```c
        case 2:
            sell_painting ();
            break;

        case 3:
            report ();
            break;

        case 4:
            done = TRUE;
            break;

        default:
            printf ("\n\nChoice is out of range\n\n");
            printf ("    Press <ENTER> to return to menu...");
            press_enter ();
            break;

        }
    }
} /* main_menu */
```

/*--------------------------------------------------------------------------------------------*/

```c
void main (void)
{
    initialize ();

    /*
     * rather than using system date, user enters it to make prototype more portable
     */
    printf ("Enter today's date (mm/dd/yy): ");
    gets (current_date);

    main_menu ();
} /* main */
```

/*--------------------------------------------------------------------------------------------*/

# CHAPTER 8

# SPECIFICATION PHASE

In this chapter, three approaches to specification are compared: formal, semiformal, and informal. I feel that students should be exposed to as many formal methods as possible. One way to introduce the FSM material to students who have had no prior exposure to formal machines is to describe a menu-based product with which most students are familiar such as a popular word-processing package on a personal computer. Point out that each menu corresponds to a state, and each menu choice to an input. Once students appreciate that they have been dealing with finite state machines for years, Section 8.6 is easy to teach.

Students who have taken an operating systems course may well have been exposed to Petri nets. Also, the basic concept can be easily understood by most of the class without much effort by the instructor. I believe that Section 8.7 should be covered, if only to ensure that students are exposed to Petri nets. However, not all students will be able to do Problem 8.13.

On the other hand, I teach Sections 8.8 and 8.9 to only graduate students. Furthermore, there is only one problem involving Z at the end of the chapter.

## PROBLEM SOLUTIONS

8.1: Both constraints superficially appear to be precise and scientific, but neither can be measured or tested. Specifically,
   (i)   The term "significantly" is imprecise—significant for whom, client or developer? Also, this is a reason for developing the product, not a constraint.
   (ii)  The term "reasonable" is imprecise—reasonable for whom, client or developer?

8.2: *Ambiguities:*
Is a clove or a head of garlic to be used?
What operations are to be performed the night before? Everything?
Which juice is to be strained, orange or lemon?
What is to be frozen, the lemon or just the juice?
Is the onion to be diced, or just the shallots?
Which mixture is to be blended for 10 minutes?
Does "blend" mean "mix by hand" or "use an electric blender?"
How are the lumps to be removed, with a strainer or a blender?
The lumps in the mixture could be the mushrooms.
Two mixtures are specified, the pockwester is added to only one of them: which?
How can you kill a "fresh" pockwester?
The terms "simmer," "bite-sized," and "soft to the touch" are imprecise.

We can broil for any time from 1 microsecond to 3 minutes, 59 seconds.
What is to be sprinkled with Parmesan—the serving platter, or the pockwester?

*Omissions:*
How large is a "large onion"?
What size can of orange juice?
How large a lemon?
What kind of bread for the crumbs?
How much flour?
How much milk?
How large are medium-sized shallots?
How large are medium-sized eggplants?
What size pockwester?
What size garlic?
How much Parmesan cheese?
What size eggs?
The sugar is not listed in the ingredients.
Nor are the mushrooms.
Nor are the frobs.
What size platter is to be used?

*Contradictions:*
The ingredients call for frozen orange juice, the recipe calls for fresh.
After the lemon has been squeezed the night before, it is then supposed to be sliced.
We are told to "stir vigorously," "slice," and "in the meantime" to coat, dip, etc.—it is impossible to do all these things at once.

*The following items are certainly confusing, but they are not ambiguities, omissions, or contradictions:*
The lemon juice, eggplant, and garlic are never used.
Grilling in a skillet is not usually a good idea.
Shaking up mushrooms wet with milk in a paper bag is fraught with difficulties.
The instruction to whisk the eggs should precede the instruction to add them to a mixture.
If the blending is to be done with an electric blender, then 10 minutes seems to be too long.
The recipe calls for first coating the mushrooms in flour, and then dipping them in milk; this may be unorthodox, but then so is much of the rest of the recipe!
Two mixtures are specified, the pockwester is added to only one of them; nothing is mentioned regarding what is to be done with the other one.

8.3: If actual sales for the current month are less than the target sales for the current month, then check whether the percentage difference between the actual sales and the target sales for the current month is 5% or more. If so, then check whether the percentage difference between the actual sales and target sales for the current month is greater than or equal to half of the percentage difference between the actual sales and target sales for the previous month. If this second condition also holds, then print a report. Otherwise, do nothing.

8.4: For each shop, the actual sales for each month are compared with the target sales for that month.

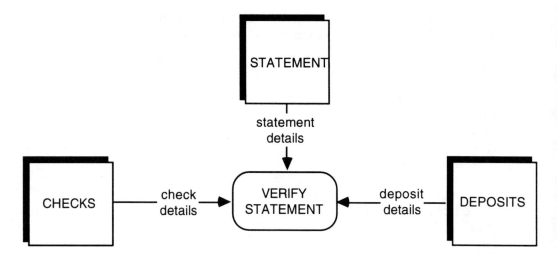

Figure 8.1. Data flow diagram for determining whether bank statement is correct.

The *effectiveness* of a given shop for a given month is defined by

$$\text{Effectiveness} = \frac{\text{actual sales}}{\text{target sales}} \times 100\%$$

The *shortfall* for a given shop for a given month is defined by

$$\text{Shortfall} = \begin{cases} 0\% & \text{if effectiveness} \geq 100\% \\ \\ 100\% - \text{effectiveness} & \text{otherwise} \end{cases}$$

A shop is deemed to have achieved its objective for the current month if the shortfall for the current month is less than or equal to 5%, or if the shortfall for the current month is less than or equal to half the shortfall for the previous month; in the case of January, the shortfall for the previous month is deemed to be 0%.

If a shop has not achieved its objective, then a report is to be printed.

8.5:    The following assumptions are made: there are no service charges, no ATM withdrawals. The only transactions that are allowed are checks and deposits. Every check bears a number. The user has a pile of canceled checks, and a pile of deposit slips.

Sort the checks in check-number order. For each check, find an entry in the bank statement that matches the check number. If no such entry is found, the statement is in error. Otherwise, mark that entry, and verify that the amount for that entry is the same as that on the check. If the amounts do not match, then the statement is in error.

Sort the deposit slips according to date of deposit. For each deposit slip, find an entry in the statement that matches the date of deposit and the amount of the deposit. Mark that entry. If no such entry is found, the statement is in error.

After all checks and deposits have been processed, verify that all items on the statement have been marked. If not, the statement is in error.

Add the amount of all deposits to the beginning balance, and from that sum subtract the sum of all the checks. If the result of that subtraction is not equal to the ending balance then the statement is in error, otherwise it is correct.

8.6:    See Figure 8.1.

8.7:    This product is concerned with books, borrowers, and librarians. The library has a collection of books which borrowers may check out and subsequently return. Each book has a unique book number. Affixed to each book is a label bearing that number in bar code format.

Each borrower has a unique borrower number. Each borrower has a card bearing that number in bar-code format that is scanned when the borrower checks out a book. Borrowers may determine all the books by a particular author in the library collection by going to a terminal and entering A = <author-name>, all the books with a specific title by entering T = <book-title>, or all the books in a particular subject area by entering S = <subject-area>.

Librarians check out a book by entering C at a terminal, scanning the borrower bar code, and scanning the book bar code. If the book is not being held for another reader, it is issued to the borrower. When a book is returned by a borrower, the librarian enters R at a terminal, and scans the book bar code. To add a new book to the collection, the librarian enters + (plus sign), the number of the new book, and other book details. To remove a book from the collection, the librarian enters – (minus sign) and enters the book number (bar-code input is inappropriate—the book may have been stolen). A librarian can put a hold on a book for a borrower by entering H = <book number> and scanning the borrower's bar code. [The need for the borrower's number was intentionally omitted from the problem statement; students should not thoughtlessly rewrite the problem statement in more formal terms, but actually consider the implications of what they are writing!] A book may not be held if it is already being held for another borrower.

8.8:    See Figure 8.2.

8.9:    *Step 1. Draw DFD.* See previous problem.

*Step 2. Decide what sections to computerize, and how.* Computerize complete product as shown in DFD, online. DFD does not show functions like issuing new borrower with an ID number and card, or maintaining borrower details. These functions were not included in the specifications, and it is therefore assumed that they will be performed manually.

*Step 3. Details of data flows.*

```
book_id
        book_number

book_details
        book_number
        book_bibilographic_details
```

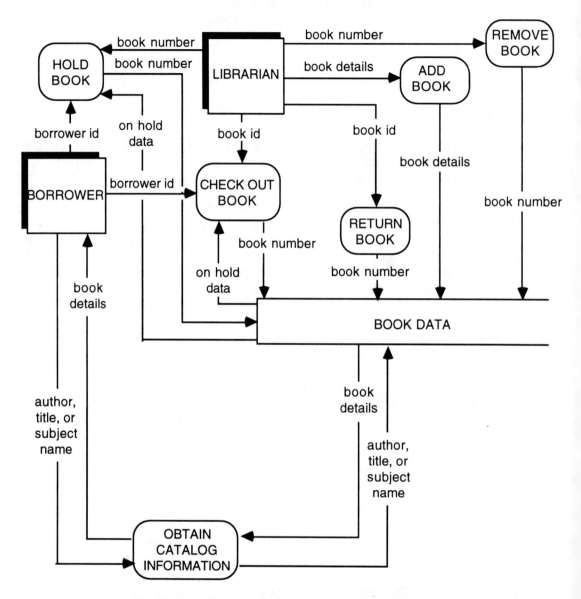

Figure 8.2. Data flow diagram for library circulation.

      author
      title
      subject
      other_details
borrower_id
    borrower_number

on_hold_data
    borrower_number if book is on hold for another borrower, else 0

*Step 4. Define logic of processes.*

ADD_BOOK

Place book_details in BOOK DATA

CHECK_OUT_BOOK
        Read book_id, borrower_id
        Check that book is not being held for another borrower
        Update BOOK DATA with borrower_id

HOLD_BOOK
        Read book_number, borrower_id
        Check if book is already on hold
        If not, update BOOK DATA to reflect borrower_id

OBTAIN_CATALOG_INFORMATION
        Read borrower's query
        Search BOOK DATA
        Answer borrower's query

REMOVE_BOOK
        Read book_number
        Delete book_details from BOOK DATA

RETURN_BOOK
        Read book_number
        Update BOOK DATA

*Step 5. Define data stores.*

BOOK DATA (512 bytes—assumption)
        book_number
        author
        title
        subject
        other_details
        on_hold_data
        borrower_number (0 if book is not checked out)

Indexed by book_number (primary), and also by author, title, and subject (secondary)

*Step 6. Define physical resources.*

BOOK DATA
        Indexed sequential file
        Primary index book_number
        Secondary indexes author, title, and subject

*Step 7. Determine input/output specifications.*

book_id, borrower_id are input with bar code wand

book_number, book_details are input at terminal

Input screens will be designed for add_book, remove_book, obtain_catalog_information

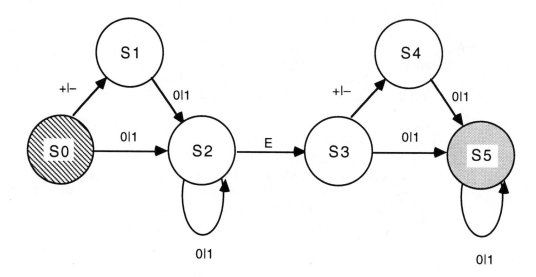

Figure 8.3. Finite state machine for accepting fixed point numbers.

Acknowledgment messages will be designed for add_book, check_out_book, remove_book, hold_book, return_book

Output screens will be designed for obtain_catalog_information

*Step 8. Perform sizing.* Assuming a maximum of 500,000 books, BOOK DATA will need to have 256 megabytes for the catalog itself, and another 25 megabytes for indexes. A further 2 megabytes will be needed for software.

*Step 9. Determine hardware requirements.*

CPU
400 megabyte disk
Tape backup system
Two terminals for borrowers
Two terminals for librarians

8.10: The FSM is shown in Figure 8.3.

Set of states is {S0, S1, S2, S3, S4, S5}.
Set of inputs is {+, −, 0, 1, E}.
The transition function is depicted on the next page.
Initial state is S0.
Set of final states is {S5}.

8.11: The FSM for the library circulation system is shown in Figure 8.4.

Set of states is {NEW BOOK, REMOVED, ON SHELVES, CHECKED OUT, ON HOLD, RETURNED AND HELD}.
Set of inputs is {C, H, R, +, −}.
The transition function is depicted below.
Initial state is NEW BOOK.
Set of final states is {REMOVED}.

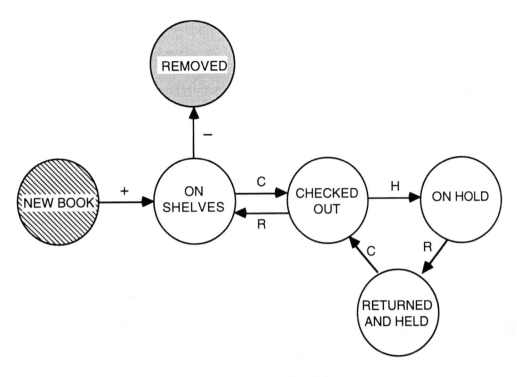

Figure 8.4. FSM for library circulation system.

8.12: The user first keys in the book_number of the book in question. A menu then appears, corresponding to the current state of the book. For example, if the book is CHECKED OUT, then the menu offers three choices, corresponding to operations R and H, and EXIT. If the user enters R, say, then a new menu appears corresponding to state ON SHELVES. If the user now enters EXIT, then the next time the product is used with respect to the same book it will be in state ON SHELVES, and the ON SHELVES menu will appear.

8.13 See Figure 8.5.

8.14 Answers will vary from enthusiasm about being given the opportunity to implement formal specifications, to dank despair at the very thought of having to implement formal specifications!

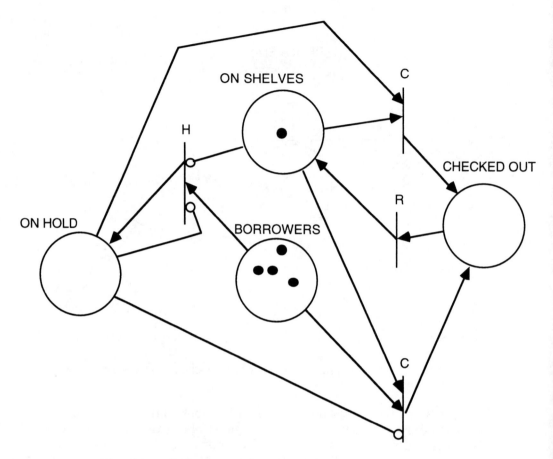

Figure 8.5. Petri net specification of library circulation system.

## TERM PROJECT

8.15 The project has been successfully defined in a number of ways. Because of the widespread use of structured systems analysis, a solution using Gane and Sarsen's method is now given.

*Step 1. Draw the Data Flow Diagram:* See Figure 8.6.

*Step 2. Decide what Sections to Computerize and How:*

Because the client will be using the product on a portable computer in order to decide on prospective purchases at remote sites, the complete product should be computerized and operate online.

*Step 3. Put in the Details of the Data Flows:*

buy painting information
      first name of artist           (21 characters)
      last name of artist            (21 characters)

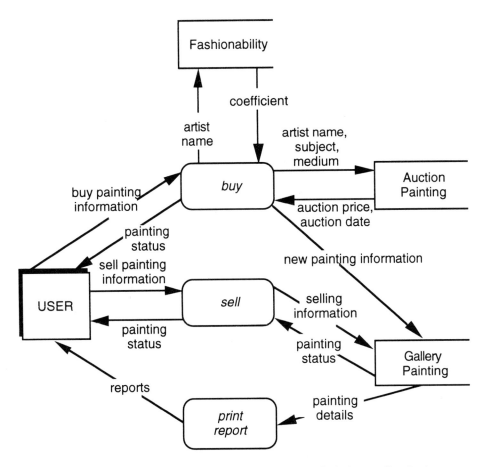

Figure 8.6. Data flow diagram for the Osbert Oglethorpe Product.

| | |
|---|---|
| title | (41 characters) |
| date of work | (9 characters) |
| medium | (10 characters) |
| subject | (10 characters) |
| height | (4 + 2 digits) |
| width | (4 + 2 digits) |
| classification | (11 characters) |

new painting information
  buy painting information (see above)

| | |
|---|---|
| date of purchase | (9 characters) |
| name of seller | (21 characters) |
| address of seller | (25 characters) |
| maximum purchase price | (3 + 2 digits) |
| actual purchase price | (3 + 2 digits) |

sell painting information

| | |
|---|---|
| first name of artist | (21 characters) |
| last name of artist | (21 characters) |
| title | (41 characters) |

selling information
    sell painting information (see above)

| | |
|---|---|
| target selling price | (3 + 2 digits) |
| date of sale | (9 characters) |
| name of buyer | (21 characters) |
| address of buyer | (25 characters) |
| actual selling price | (3 + 2 digits) |

painting details

| | |
|---|---|
| last name of artist | (21 characters) |
| title | (41 characters) |
| classification | (11 characters) |
| date of purchase | (9 characters) |
| maximum purchase price | (3 + 2 digits) |
| actual purchase price | (3 + 2 digits) |
| target selling price | (3 + 2 digits) |
| date of sale | (9 characters) |
| actual selling price | (3 + 2 digits) |

painting status

| | |
|---|---|
| status | (6 characters) |

reports
    painting details (see above)

report type

| | |
|---|---|
| type | (7 characters) |

## Step 4. *Define the Logic of the Processes:*

BUY
    If painting already purchased, print error message,
    else
        compute maximum purchase price.
        If maximum purchase price > 0
            Get purchase information.
            Add new painting to GALLERY PAINTING.

SELL
    Get selling information.
    If painting not already purchased, print error message,
    else
        if painting already sold, print error message
        else
            add new sale information to GALLERY PAINTING.

PRINT REPORT
    For each GALLERY PAINTING object that has been processed over the past year,
        if the object satisfies the conditions of report type, print object information.

*Step 5.  Define the Data Stores:*

AUCTION PAINTING
    first name of artist        (21 characters)
    last name of artist        (21 characters)
    title        (41 characters)
    date of work        (9 characters)
    medium        (10 characters)
    subject        (10 characters)
    height        (4 + 2 digits)
    width        (4 + 2 digits)
    auction date        (9 characters)
    auction price        (3 + 2 digits)

FASHIONABILITY
    first name of artist        (21 characters)
    last name of artist        (21 characters)
    coefficient        (4 + 2 digits)

GALLERY PAINTING
    first name of artist        (21 characters)
    last name of artist        (21 characters)
    title        (41 characters)
    date of work        (9 characters)
    medium        (10 characters)
    subject        (10 characters)
    height        (4 + 2 digits)
    width        (4 + 2 digits)
    classification        (11 characters)
    date of purchase        (9 characters)
    name of seller        (21 characters)
    address of seller        (25 characters)
    maximum purchase price        (3 + 2 digits)
    actual purchase price        (3 + 2 digits)
    target selling price        (3 + 2 digits)
    date of sale        (9 characters)
    name of buyer        (21 characters)
    address of buyer        (25 characters)
    actual selling price        (3 + 2 digits)

All files are sequential, and hence there is no DIAD.

*Step 6.  Define the Physical Resources:*

AUCTION PAINTING
    Sequential file
    Stored on disk

FASHIONABILITY
    Sequential file
    Stored on disk

GALLERY PAINTING
    Sequential file
    Stored on disk

*Step 7. Determine the Input/Output Specifications:*

Input screens will be designed for the following processes:
    get gallery description, buy painting, sell painting, update fashionability coefficient

The following reports will be displayed:
    list of bought paintings, list of sold paintings, current fashion trends

The screens and reports of the rapid prototype will be used as a basis for the above.


*Step 8. Perform Sizing:*

Approximately 4 megabytes of storage are needed for the software. Each gallery painting object will require approximately 500 bytes of storage. Thus, approximately 0.5 megabytes of secondary storage are needed for every 1,000 paintings in the gallery.


*Step 9. Determine the Hardware Requirements:*

486 33Mhz portable computer.
300 megabyte hard disk.
Cartridge tape for backup.
Laser printer for printing reports.

# CHAPTER 9

## OBJECT-ORIENTED ANALYSIS PHASE

The exercises in this chapter give students their first practical exposure to the object-oriented paradigm. It is important to stress that repeated iteration is an intrinsic quality of this paradigm, and of object-oriented analysis (OOA) in particular. In particular, problems 9.2 and 9.4 seem extremely straightforward. However, the students will have to iterate a number of times between class modeling, dynamic modeling, and functional modeling before they arrive at an acceptable solution.

## PROBLEM SOLUTIONS

9.1:    The dynamic models for classes **Button, Elevator, Elevator_Doors,** and **Request_ Database** are shown in Figures 9.1, 9.2, 9.3, and 9.4, respectively.

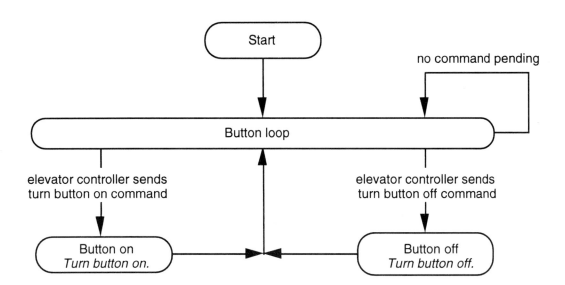

Figure 9.1. Dynamic model for class Button.

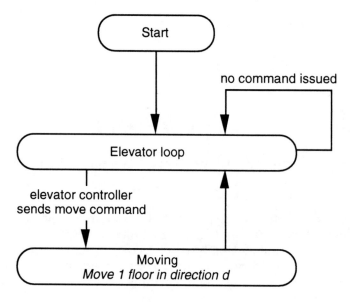

Figure 9.2. Dynamic model for class Elevator.

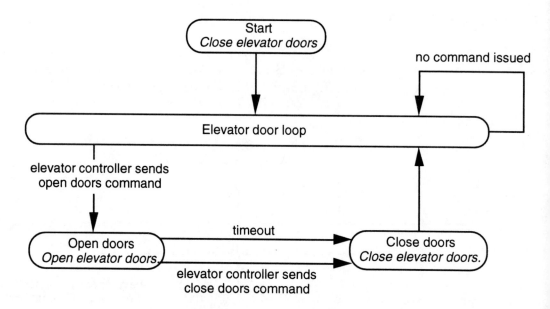

Figure 9.3. Dynamic model for class Elevator_Doors.

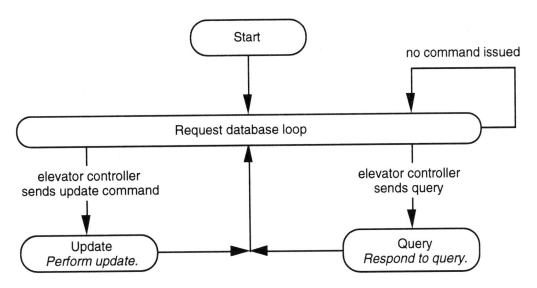

Figure 9.4. Dynamic model for class Request_Database.

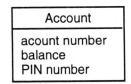

Figure 9.5. Class model for ATM product.

9.2:     *Class Modeling*

*Stage 1. Concise Problem Definition:* A system to control an automatic teller machine (ATM) is to be constructed.

*Stage 2. Informal Strategy:* A system to control an ATM is to be constructed. After a customer's card has been successfully verified, the customer may deposit and withdraw money from an account, inquire about the balance of an account, and transfer funds between two separate accounts.

*Stage 3. Formalize the Strategy:* A **system** to control an **ATM** is to be constructed. After a **customer's card** has been successfully verified, the **customer** may deposit and withdraw **money** from an **account**, inquire about the **balance** of an **account**, and transfer **funds** between two separate **accounts**.

With regard to the nouns in the previous paragraph, **ATM**, **card**, and **customer** do not change while the system is operating; in object-oriented terminology, they do not have an internal state. Also, **funds** and **money** are abstract nouns. Finally, **balance** is a property of **account**. Thus, the sole candidate class is **Account**.

The class model is shown in Figure 9.5.

62

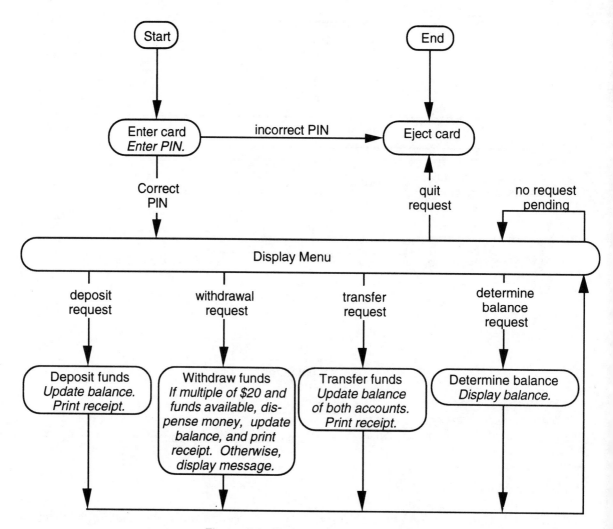

Figure 9.6. Dynamic model for ATM product.

*Dynamic Modeling*

See Figure 9.6.

*Functional Modeling*

See Figure 9.7.

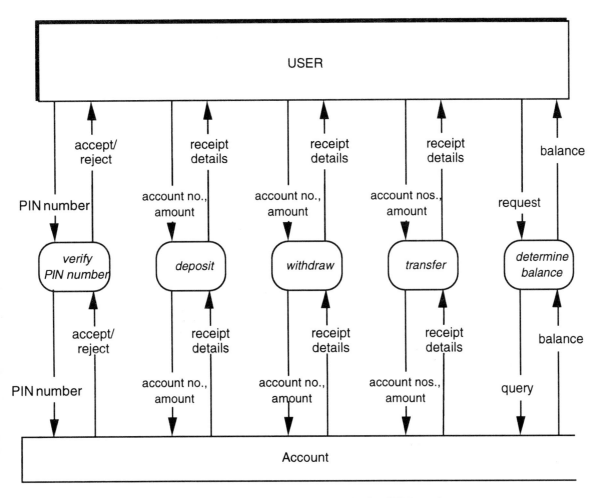

Figure 9.7. Functional model for ATM product.

9.3:      As explained in Section 8.6 of *Classical and Object-Oriented Software Engineering*, an FSM is a quintuple. In nonmathematical terms, an FSM consists of states, and the inputs that result in a transition from state to state. For object-oriented modeling, however, we also want to incorporate the action that is to be taken when entering a state. Furthermore, this should appear as part of the diagram that represents the dynamic model. This simplifies later development, particularly the object-oriented design phase. However, the resulting formalism will not be formal, a price we are willing to pay because OOA as a whole is a semi-formal technique.

9.4:      *Class Modeling*

*Stage 1. Concise Problem Definition:* An automated library circulation system is to be constructed.

*Stage 2. Informal Strategy:* An automated library circulation system is to be constructed. Each book in the library, as well as each borrower, can be identified by a barcode. A book can be checked out provided it is not being held for another borrower; at most one borrower can place a hold on a book checked out by another borrower. When a book is returned, it is checked in by a librarian. Borrowers and librarians are

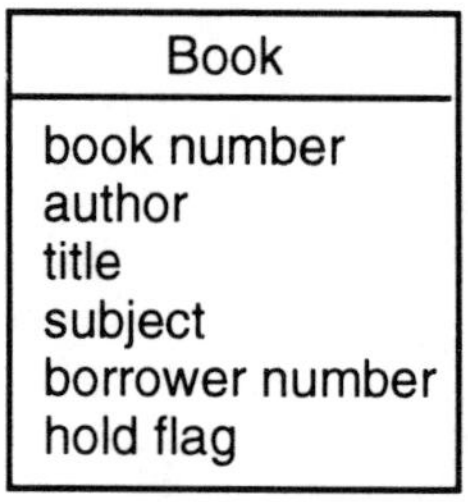

64

```
┌─────────────────────────┐
│          Book           │
├─────────────────────────┤
│  book number            │
│  author                 │
│  title                  │
│  subject                │
│  borrower number        │
│  hold flag              │
└─────────────────────────┘
```

Figure 9.8. Class model for library circulation system.

permitted to query a catalog of library holdings. Librarians may also modify the catalog.

*Stage 3. Formalize the Strategy:* An automated library circulation system is to be constructed. Each book in the library, as well as each borrower, can be identified by a bar-code. A book can be checked out provided it is not being held for another borrower; at most one borrower can place a hold on a book checked out by another borrower. When a book is returned, it is checked in by a librarian. Borrowers and librarians are permitted to query a catalog of library holdings. Librarians may also modify the catalog.

With regard to the nouns in the previous paragraph, borrower, librarian, and bar-code do not change while the library is operating; in object-oriented terminology, they do not have an internal state. Accordingly, these nouns cannot correspond to classes. In addition, library, hold, holding, and system are abstract nouns. Finally, catalog is information that relates to books. This leaves Book as the sole candidate class.

The class model is shown in Figure 9.8.

*Dynamic Modeling*

See Figure 9.9.

*Functional Modeling*

See Figure 9.10.

65

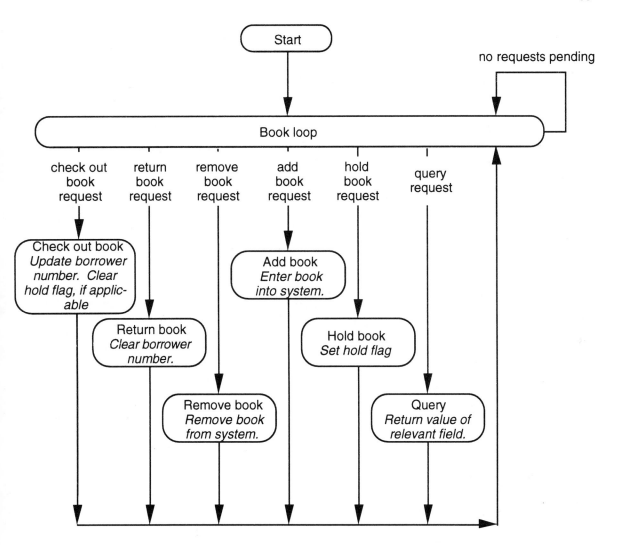

Figure 9.9. Dynamic model for library circulation system.

66

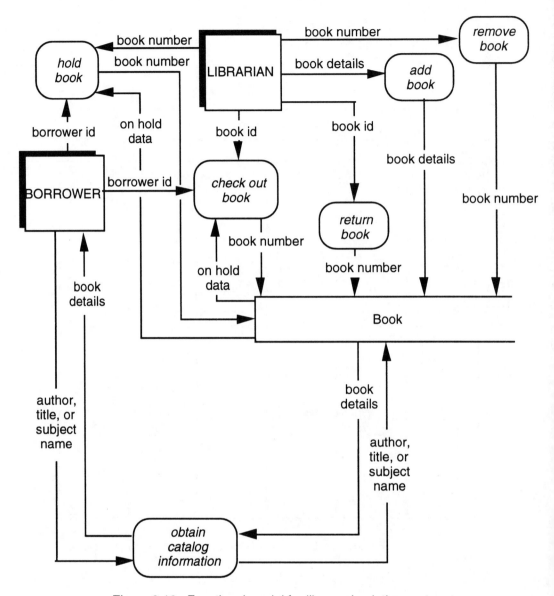

Figure 9.10. Functional model for library circulation system.

9.5: It is possible, in theory, to do the functional modeling stage before the class modeling stage. However, this is not advisable, because when the classes are eventually extracted, major changes in the functional model are almost certain to be required. The reason is that the functional model (essentially a data flow diagram) cannot represent or identify inheritance.

9.6: It is possible (though not advisable) to use the rapid prototype as a way of determining what the classes should be.

9.7: A wide variety of formalisms could be used, both graphical and textual. All that is required is that the formalism should reflect the various states, transactions, and actions involved.

However, such formalisms are less convenient to use; for example, in the solution to Problem 9.3 we pointed out that the formalism of Chapter 8 is less suitable than the one used here. Textual formalisms are even less suitable.

9.8: In the real world, they both involve flowing water. The important metaphor, with respect to software development, is that the movement of water in a waterfall is strictly from the top to the bottom while the movement of water in a fountain may alternate between moving up and down. That is to say, in a fountain the water is initially forced upward but eventually descends, possibly making contact with other water molecules as they ascend.

The two software models both cover the same phases, from requirements analysis to maintenance. The difference lies in the manner in which these phases are carried out. The fountain model allows (or even encourages) some phases to be performed in parallel, whereas no phase of the waterfall model can be started before the previous phase has been completed. A second difference is that the fountain model supports iteration within each phase.

9.9: The principle of stepwise refinement requires as many decisions as possible to be postponed. All the operations that have to be included in the product appear in the dynamic model. However, organizing those operations into methods and then assigning the methods to specific classes can wait until the design phase. On the other hand, modeling becomes extremely complex unless the attributes are assigned to their specific classes.

In fact, there is another good reason to wait until the design phase before allocating methods to classes, namely that the choice of architecture (e.g., client-server) will affect where the classes are physically located, and hence may affect how the operations are organized into methods, and which methods should be allocated to which classes.

## TERM PROJECT

9.10: *Class Modeling*

*Concise Problem Definition:* A computerized system is needed to improve the decision-making process for purchasing works of art.

*Informal Strategy:* Monthly reports are to be generated in order to document the efficacy of the decision-making process for purchasing works of art. The reports contain buying and selling information about paintings which are classified as masterpieces, masterworks, and other.

*Formalize the Strategy:* Monthly **reports** are to be generated in order to document the efficacy of the decision-making **process** for purchasing **works** of **art**. The **reports**

68

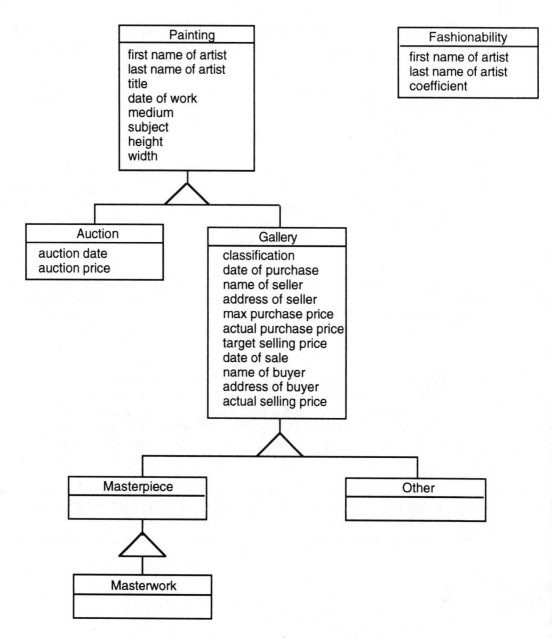

Figure 9.11. Class model for Osbert Oglesby product.

contain buying and selling information about paintings which are classified as masterpieces, masterworks, and other.

After removing the abstract nouns from the above paragraph, the candidate classes are: Painting, Masterpiece, Masterwork, and Other.

The class model is shown in Figure 9.11.

*Dynamic Modeling*

See Figure 9.12.

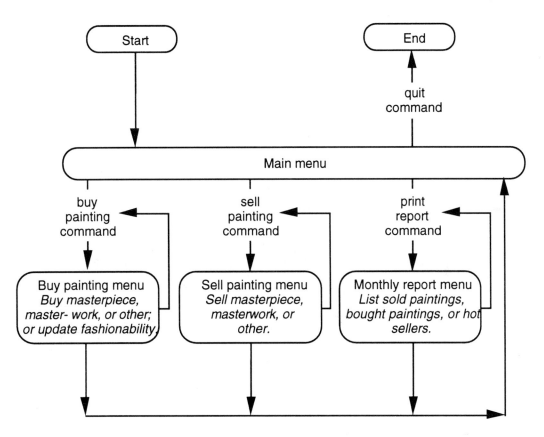

Figure 9.12. Dynamic model for Osbert Oglesby product.

70

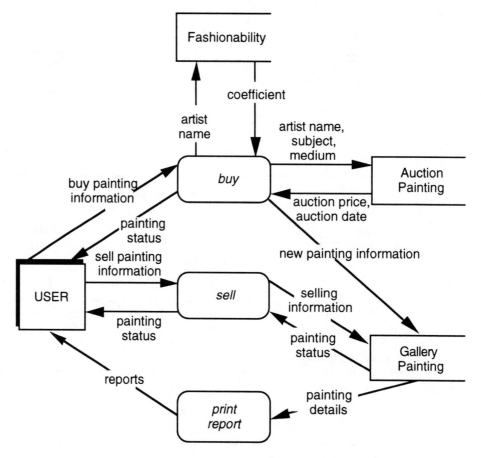

Figure 9.13. Functional model for Osbert Oglesby product.

*Functional Modeling*

See Figure 9.13.

# CHAPTER 10

# PLANNING PHASE

The major pedagogic problem I have had with this chapter is convincing students that the material in Chapter 10 is essential for a software engineer to know. After all, students at this stage of their college careers have been successfully programming for three years or more without drawing up a plan of any sort. This is one of the places in the course where I draw a clear distinction between programming and software engineering, and point out that the former is a very small subset of the latter.

## PROBLEM SOLUTIONS

10.1: A "millstone" is a heavy burden; some organizations have difficulties meeting milestones at the promised time.

10.2:  (i)  From Equation (10.1), size $S = Fi + Fl + Pr = 17 + 61 + 89 = 167$

   (ii)  From Equation (10.2), cost $C = b \times S = 793 \times 167 = \$132,431$

   (iii)  Productivity $= (132,431 - 127,000) / 132,431$ or 4.1% higher than the company average.

10.3:  From Figure 10.1 of *Classical and Object-Oriented Software Engineering*,

$$UFP = 6 \times 3 + 7 \times 4 + 10 \times 6 + 7 \times 5 + 41 \times 3 + 11 \times 10 + 21 \times 10 = 584$$

10.4:  From Equation (10.4), $TCF = 0.65 + 0.01 \times 57 = 1.22$.

Using Equation (10.5), $FP = UFP \times TCF = 584 \times 1.22 = 712$

10.5:  It is easy to measure, either manually or using a simple CASE tool. But more importantly, it is easy for management to comprehend.

10.6:  Using Equation (10.7) for an embedded mode product

$$\text{Nominal effort} = 2.8 \times 75^{1.20} = 498 \text{ person-months}$$

Product of multipliers is

$$1.00 \text{ (nominal)} \times 1.16 \text{ (database size)} \times 1.10 \text{ (use of software tools)} = 1.28$$

Estimated effort is then

Nominal effort × product of multipliers = 498 × 1.28 = 637 person-months

10.7: Nominal effort (organic mode) = $3.2 \times 35^{1.05}$ = 134 person-months

Multiplier for $P_1$ = 1.65
Multiplier for $P_2$ = 0.70

Multiplier for team A = $0.71 \times 0.82 \times 0.70 \times 0.90 \times 0.95$ = 0.35
Multiplier for team B = $1.46 \times 1.29 \times 1.42 \times 1.21 \times 1.14$ = 3.69

(i) If team A develops $P_1$, total effort = $134 \times 1.65 \times 0.35$ = 77 person-months.
If team B develops $P_2$, total effort = $134 \times 0.70 \times 3.69$ = 346 person-months.

Total = 423 person-months

(ii) If team B develops $P_1$, total effort = $134 \times 1.65 \times 3.69$ = 816 person-months.
If team A develops $P_2$, total effort = $134 \times 0.70 \times 0.35$ = 33 person-months.

Total = 849 person-months.

(iii) Assignment (i) makes more sense, and is backed by the COCOMO predictions.

10.8: Nominal effort for this organic mode product is $3.2 \times 42^{1.05}$ = 162 person months

(i) At $8200 per person-month, project costs $1,328,400.

(ii) Replacing the staff with team A from Problem 10.7, the cost for the project becomes $(162 \times 0.35) \times 10,800$ = $612,360, or a gain of $716,040.

10.9: First obtain independent COCOMO and function point estimates as a check. Assuming that the predictions do not change, the next step is to discuss the product with experienced software engineers, and ask them to come up with estimates based on their experience ("expert judgment by analogy"). Use their estimates to try to decide whether the COCOMO or function point estimator is more likely to be an accurate predictor of the cost of the product. If this, too, fails, then use the function point estimate on the grounds that it is generally less damaging in the long run to overestimate than to underestimate cost.

10.10: From Equation (10.8), $R_C = \dfrac{t}{k^2} e^{-t^2/2k^2}$.

Take the derivative of $R_C$ with respect to $t$, and set it to zero. This yields

$$\frac{dR_C}{dt} = \frac{1}{k^2}\left\{ e^{-t^2/2k^2} + t \times \left(\frac{-2t}{2k^2}\right) e^{-t^2/2k^2} \right\} = 0$$

Solving for $t$ gives the result $t = \pm k$. To show that $t = k$ is a maximum, take the second derivative of $R_C$, and set $t = k$. This yields

$$\frac{d^2 R_C}{dt^2}\Big|_{t=k} = \frac{-2}{k^3\sqrt{e}} < 0 \text{ as required}$$

Maximum resource consumption is then $\dfrac{1}{k\sqrt{e}}$

10.11: Although it is true that every product is maintained, the maintenance need not be performed by the organization that is responsible for the development.

# TERM PROJECT

10.12: The solution presented here is an SPMP for development of the OOAD product by a small software organization consisting of three individuals, namely Pat, the owner of the company, and two software engineers, Rob and Mary. The Instructor's Manual for the First Edition of *Software Engineering* (available from Irwin) contains an SPMP for a project developed by a large software organization.

*1. Introduction.*

*1.1. Project Overview.* The objective of this project is to develop a software product that will assist Osbert Oglesby, Art Dealer (OOAD) in making decisions regarding the purchase of paintings to be displayed and sold in his gallery. The product will allow the client to buy and sell masterpieces, masterworks, and other paintings. The product will perform the required calculations and record-keeping on these paintings, and produce reports listing bought paintings, sold paintings, and current fashion trends.

The time, budget, and personnel requirements are as follows:

      Requirements phase (1 week, two team members, $1690)
      Object-oriented analysis phase (1 week, two team members, $1690)
      Planning phase (1 week, two team members, $1690)
      Design phase (2 weeks, two team members, $3380)
      Implementation phase (3 weeks, three team members, $7600)
      Integration phase (2 weeks, three team members, $5070)

[In practice, the implementation and integration phases are combined, as described in Chapter 13.]

The total development time is 10 weeks and the total internal cost is $21,120.

*1.2. Project Deliverables.* The complete source code with user and operations manuals will be delivered 10 weeks after the project commences. The client will be responsible for acquiring the recommended hardware and system software by the time the product is delivered.

*1.3. Evolution of the SPMP.* All changes in the SPMP must be agreed to by Pat before they are implemented. All changes should be documented in order to keep the SPMP correct and up to date.

*1.4. Reference materials.* Our company coding, documentation, and testing standards.

*1.5 Definitions and Acronyms.*
  OOAD—Osbert Oglesby, Art Dealer; Mr. Oglesby is our client
  SPMP—software project management plan

## 2. Project Organization.

*2.1. Process Model.* The software life-cycle model to be used is the waterfall model with rapid prototyping. The specifications were written by Rob and Mary, and verified by the client at meetings between Pat and the client. The design task will be shared between Rob and Mary, and Pat will check the overall design. Coding will also be performed by Rob and Mary. Rob and Mary will test each other's code and Pat will conduct integration testing. Extensive testing will then be done by all three. The time required for all these activities are outlined in the Introduction.

*2.2. Organizational Structure.* The development team consists of Pat (owner), Rob, and Mary (software engineers).

*2.3. Organizational Boundaries and Interfaces.* All the work on this project will be performed by Pat, Rob, and Mary. Pat will meet weekly with the client to report progress and discuss possible changes and modifications. Any major changes which will affect the milestones or the budget will have to be approved by Pat, and documented. There will be no outside SQA personnel involved. The benefits of having someone other than the individual who carried out the development task to do the testing will be accomplished by each person testing another person's work products.

*2.4. Project Responsibilities.* Each member is responsible for the quality of the module he or she codes. Pat will handle the class definitions and report modules, Rob will write the modules to handle bought paintings, and Mary will code the modules that handle sold paintings. Pat will oversee module integration and overall quality of the product and will liaise with the client.

## 3. Managerial Process.

*3.1. Managerial Objectives and Priorities.* The overall objective is to deliver a fault-free product on time and within the budget. If this cannot be achieved, priority is given to completing the routines needed to buy paintings; reports have the lowest priority.

The three team members will work separately on their assigned modules. Pat's assigned role will be to monitor the daily progress of the other two, oversee integration, be responsible for overall quality, and interact with the client. Team members will meet at the end of each day and discuss problems and progress. Formal meetings with the client will be held at the end of each week to report progress and determine if any changes need to be made. Pat will ensure that schedule and budget requirements are met. Risk management will also be Pat's responsibility.

Minimizing faults and maximizing user-friendliness will be Pat's priorities. Pat is also responsible for all documentation and has to ensure that it is up to date.

*3.2. Assumptions, Dependencies and Constraints.* Acceptance criteria are listed in the specification document. They include the following:

The deadline must be met.
The budget constraints must be met.
The product must be reliable.
The architecture must be open so that additional modules may be added later.
The product must conform to the client's hardware.
The product must be user-friendly.

*3.3. Risk Management.* The risk factors and the tracking mechanisms are as follows:

There is no existing software with which the new product can be compared. Accordingly, it will not be possible to run the product in parallel with an existing one. Therefore, the product should be subjected to extensive testing.

The client is assumed to be inexperienced with computers. Therefore, special attention should be paid to the specification phase and communication with the client. The product has to be made as user-friendly as possible.

There is always the possibility of a major design fault, so extensive testing will be done during the design phase. Also, each of the team members will initially test his or her own code and then test the code of another member. Pat will be responsible for integration testing.

The product must meet the specified storage requirements and response times. This should not be a major problem because of the small size of the product, but it will be monitored by Pat throughout development.

There is a slim chance of hardware failure, in which case another machine will be leased. If there is a fault in the compiler, it will be replaced. These are covered in the warranties received from the hardware and compiler suppliers.

*3.4. Monitoring and Controlling Mechanisms.* Pat will be responsible for all review and auditing. This will be accomplished through daily meetings with the team members. At each meeting, Rob and Mary will present the day's progress and problems. Pat will determine whether they are progressing as expected, and whether they are following the specifications and the SPMP. Any major problems faced by the team members will immediately be reported to Pat.

*3.5. Staffing Plan.* Pat is needed for the entire 10 weeks, for the first 5 weeks only in a managerial capacity and the second 5 weeks as both manager and programmer. Rob and Mary are needed for the entire 10 weeks.

*4. Technical Process.*

*4.1. Methods, Tools, and Techniques.* The waterfall model with rapid prototyping will be used (section 3.3.1). The rapid prototype was written in C. The specifications were drawn up using object-oriented analysis (Section 9.2). Object-oriented design (Section 11.8) will be used. Source code will be written in C++ and run under UNIX on a personal computer. Documentation and coding will be done in accordance with company standards.

*4.2. Software Documentation.* Software documentation will follow company standards. Reviews for documentation will be conducted by Pat at the completion of each phase of the process model. This will ensure that all the documentation for a particular phase is complete by the time the next phase is started.

*4.3. Project Support Functions.* Quality assurance will be performed as described in section 2.1.

## 5. Work Packages, Schedule, and Budget.

*5.1. Work Packages.* The objects involved, masterpieces, masterworks, and other types of paintings, are to be bought and sold. More specifically, routines are needed to store information about bought and sold paintings, while assisting the client in arriving at a maximum purchase price and a target selling price for each type of painting. In addition, reports listing bought paintings, sold paintings, and fashion trends are to be produced. The methods for each of the objects will be created independently. The team members will be in constant communication; this should ensure that the objects are compatible.

*5.2. Dependencies.* As specified in the process model. Specifically, no phase will be started until the work products of the previous phase have been approved by Pat.

*5.3. Resource Requirements.* Three personal computers running under UNIX, together with standard UNIX tools.

*5.4. Budget and Resource Allocation.* The budget for each phase is as follows:

| | |
|---|---|
| Requirements phase: | $1690 |
| Object-oriented analysis phase: | $1690 |
| Planning phase: | $1690 |
| Object-oriented design phase: | $3380 |
| Implementation phase: | $7600 |
| Integration phase: | $5070 |
| | |
| Total : | $21,120 |

*5.5. Schedule.*

| | |
|---|---|
| Week 1: | Met with client, determined requirements. Produced rapid prototype. Client and users approved rapid prototype. |
| Week 2: | Wrote specification document. Inspected specification document, approved by client. |
| Week 3: | Produced SPMP, inspected SPMP. |
| Week 4, 5: | Object-oriented design document, object-oriented design inspection, detailed design document, detailed design inspection. |
| Week 6, 7, 8: | Implementation and inspection of each module, module testing and documentation. |
| Week 9, 10: | Integration of each module, inspection of individual modules, product testing, documentation check. |

*Additional Components.*

*Security:* A password will be needed to use the product.

*Training:* Training will be done by Pat at time of delivery. Since the product is straight-forward to use, 1 day is sufficient for training. Pat will answer questions at no cost for the first year of use.

*Product Maintenance:* Corrective maintenance will be done by the team at no cost for a period of 12 months. A separate contract will be drawn up regarding enhancement.

# CHAPTER 11

# DESIGN PHASE

I suggest that at least two different techniques for architectural design be taught. It is important that students be exposed to more than one design method, otherwise they will think that there is only one way to design a product. Data flow analysis is the most popular design method today, whereas object-oriented design will surely be the design method of the future, so I recommend that those two methods be taught. At the same time, I consider that the ideas of Jackson System Development are of major theoretical importance, so if time permits this method should also be covered. Finally, transaction analysis is quick and easy to teach, and is superior to data flow analysis for the design of transaction-processing systems.

## PROBLEM SOLUTIONS

11.1: An architectural design is presented in Figure 11.1; the detailed design of one module appears in Figure 11.2.

It is advisable to inform the students whether or not a complete detailed design is required, and if not, the number of modules that should be designed.

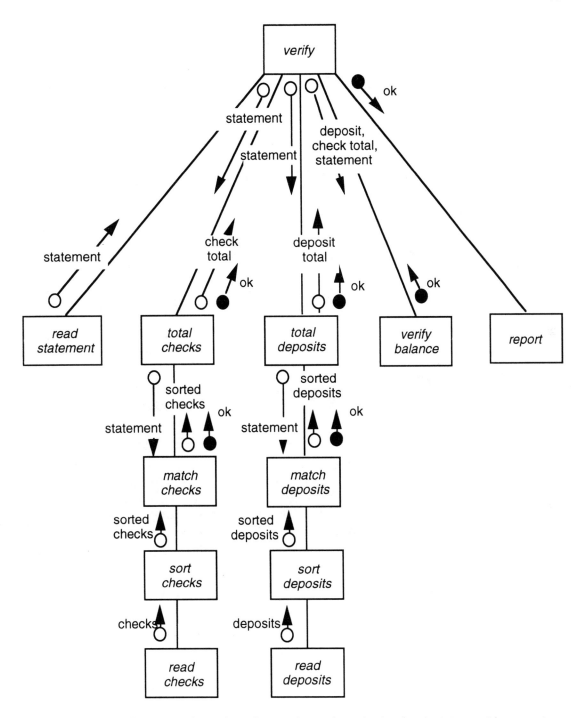

Figure 11.1. Structure chart of product to determine whether bank statement is correct.

| Module name | total checks |
|---|---|
| Module type | function, *does not return value* |
| Parameters | statement : statement type<br>check total : money type<br>ok : Boolean |
| Error messages | *None* |
| Files accessed | *None* |
| Files changed | *None* |
| Modules called | match checks<br>    *Parameters:*        statement : statement type<br>                             sorted checks : check list<br>                             ok : Boolean |
| Narrative | *This module calls match checks which returns* ok, *a Boolean, and a sorted list of checks. If the value of* ok *that is returned is* true, *then this module takes the sorted list of checks and returns the sum of the dollar values of the checks. Otherwise, this module does nothing, and returns the value of* ok, *unchanged, to its caller.* |

Figure 11.2. Detailed design of one module of product to determine whether bank statement is correct.

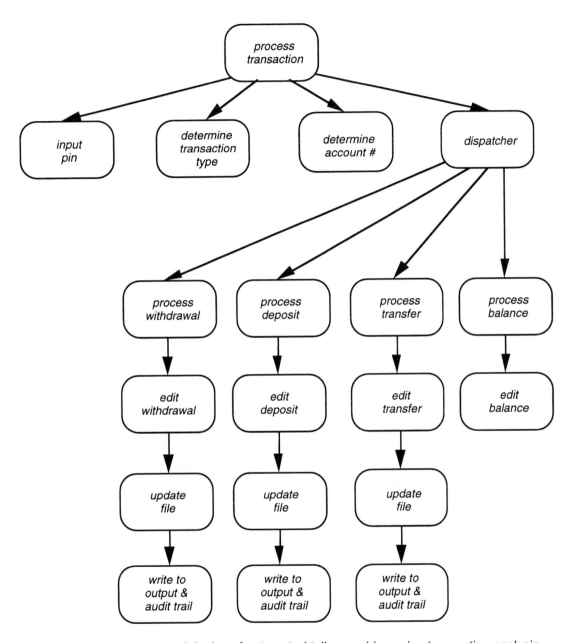

Figure 11.3. Architectural design of automated teller machine using transaction analysis.

11.2:  See Figure 11.3.

In practice, when a deposit is made the account file is updated only after the deposit has been verified.

82

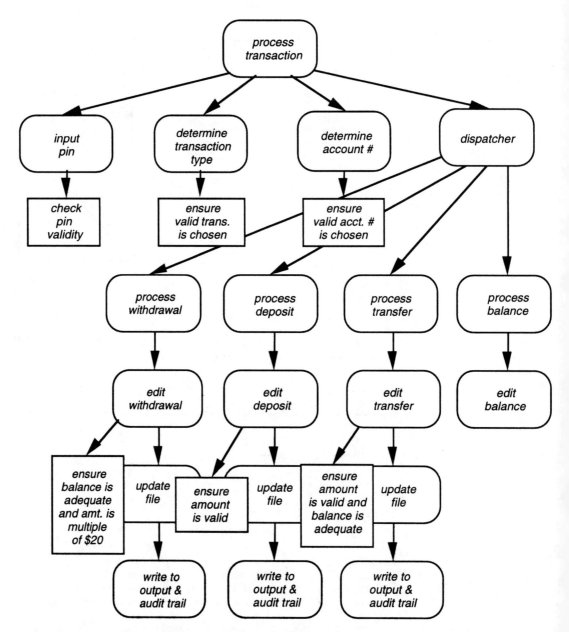

Figure 11.4.  Architectural design of automated teller machine using transaction analysis. Error-handling modules have been added.

11.3:   In the architectural design of Figure 11.4 all modules have functional cohesion, there is data coupling between each pair of communicating modules and no coupling between all other pairs.

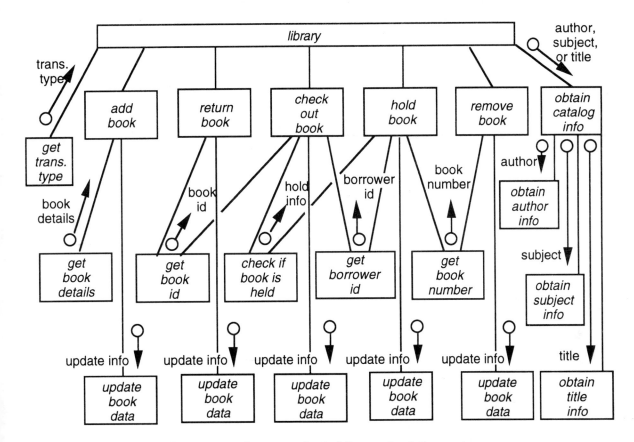

Figure 11.5. Structure chart of library circulation system.

11.4: Pseudocode is a more concise way of representing a detailed design than the tabular method. Also, coding from pseudocode is more straightforward. The disadvantage is that a carelessly designed pseudocode can be programming language-independent.

11.5: The architectural design is shown in Figure 11.5.

84

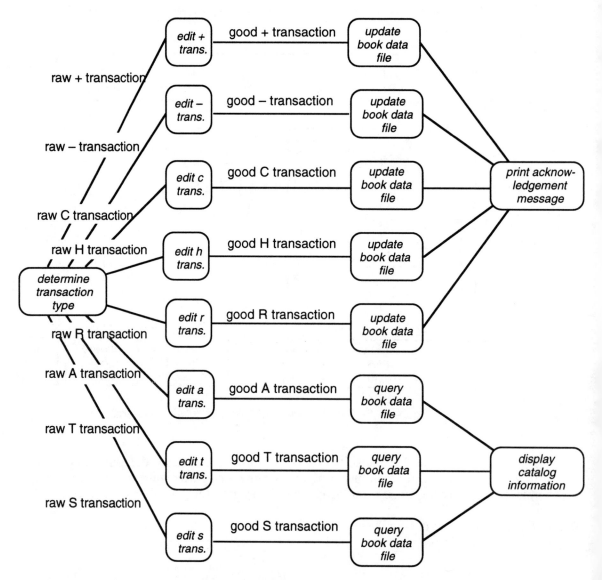

Figure 11.6. Architectural design of library circulation system using transaction analysis.

11.6: The architectural design is shown in Figure 11.6.

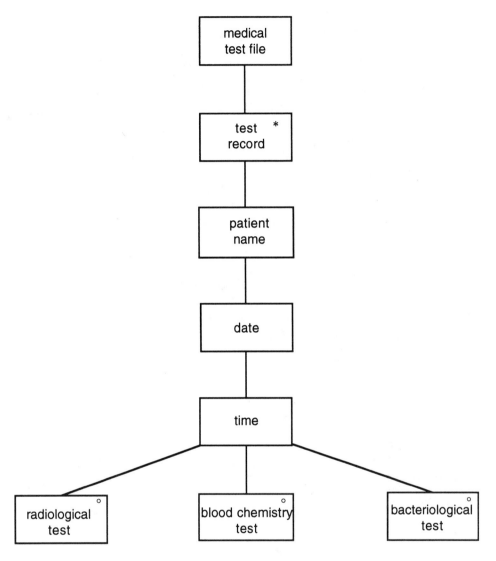

1. *For any two consecutive medical test records* t *and* t + 1,
   t.patient_name ≤ (t + 1).patient_name

2. *If* t.patient_name = (t+ 1).patient_name, *then*
   t.date ≤ (t + 1).date

3. *If* t.patient_name = (t + 1).patient_name, *and* t.date = (t + 1).date, *then*
   t.time ≤ (t + 1).time

Figure 11.7. Description of medical test file using JSD notation.

11.7: See Figure 11.7.

11.8:
```
elevator_1 seq
    getsv elevator_sv;
    light_on[1];
    at_floor[1]_body itr while (at_floor[1])
```

```
                       getsv elevator_sv;
                    at_floor[1]_body end;
                    light_off[1];
                    depart[1];
                    moving[1]_body itr while (moving)
                        getsv elevator_sv;
                    moving[1]_body end;
                    elevator_body itr
                        floor[f] seq
                            getsv elevator_sv;
                            arrive[f];
                            light_on[f];
                            at_floor[f]_body itr while (at_floor[f])
                                getsv elevator_sv;
                            at_floor[f]_body end;
                            getsv elevator_sv;
                            light_off[f];
                            depart[f];
                            moving[f]_body itr while (moving)
                                getsv elevator_sv;
                            moving[f]_body end;
                        floor[f] end;
                    elevator_body end;
                elevator_1 end;
```

11.9:   *Step 1. Entity action step:*

Entity: librarian
    Action:     add book
    Action:     remove book
    Action:     check out book to borrower
    Action:     return book to shelves
    Action:     hold book for borrower

Entity: borrower
    Action:     request to check out book
    Action:     return book to librarian
    Action:     request hold on book
    Action:     obtain catalog information

*Step 2. Entity structure step:*

Each book[i] in the library must be in one of the following states:

book[i] available
book[i] checked out
book[i] held for borrower[k]

The actions performed by or on the entities librarian and borrower are shown in Figures 11.8 and 11.9 respectively.

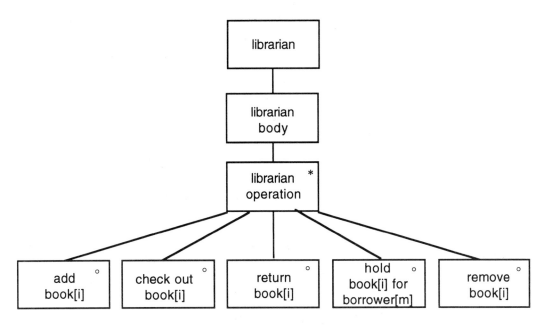

1. check out book[i], return book[i], *and* hold book[i] *can be performed on* book[i] *only if* add book[i] *has been performed, but not* remove book[i].

2. book[i] *can be held for at most one borrower.*

3. hold book[i] *can be performed only if* book[i] *is checked out and not held for borrower.*

4. borrower[k] *can borrow* book[i] *if on shelves or held for* borrower[k].

Figure 11.8.  JSD structure diagram for librarian.

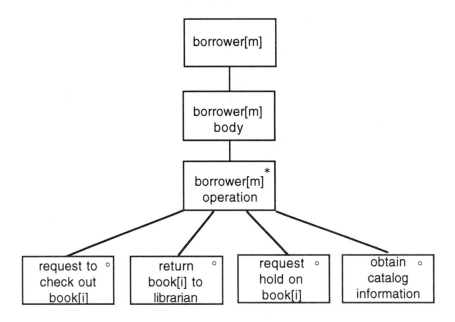

Figure 11.9  JSD structure diagram for automated library circulation system

88

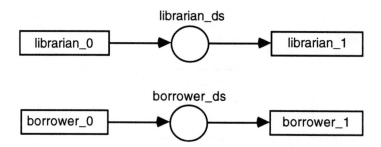

Figure 11.10. JSD structure diagrams showing connection between real-world processes and model processes

*Step 3. Initial model step:*

The mapping between the model and the real world is shown in Figure 11.10.

The structure text for librarian_1 is shown below.

```
librarian_1 seq
    librarian_body itr;
        librarian_read_and_perform_operation seq
            read librarian_ds;
            librarian_operation sel
                add_book;
            librarian_operation sel
                check_out_book[i]_body itr
                        while (available or held_for_borrower[k])
                    check_out_book[i];
                check_out_book[i]_body end;
            librarian_operation sel
                return_book[i];
            librarian_operation sel
                hold_book[i]_for_borrower[k]_body itr
                        while (checked_out and not held)
                    hold_book[i]_for_borrower[k];
                hold_book[i]_for_borrower[k]_body end;
            librarian_operation sel
                remove_book;
            librarian_operation end;
        librarian_read_and_perform_operation end;
    librarian_body end;
librarian_1 end;
```

The structure text for borrower_1 is

```
borrower_1 seq
    borrower_body itr
        borrower_read_and_perform_operation seq
            read borrow_ds;
```

```
            borrower_operation sel
                request_to_check_out_book;
            borrower_operation sel
                return_book_to_librarian itr
                        while (checked_out to borrower[k])
                    check_out_book[i];
                return_book_to_librarian end;
            borrower_operation sel
                request_hold_on_book;
            borrower_operation sel
                obtain_catalog_information;
            borrower_operation end;
        borrower_read_and_perform_operation end;
    borrower_body end;
borrower_1 end;
```

*Step 4. Function step:*

When librarian adds book[i] to collection, set state to book[i]_available. When book is checked out, set state to book[i]_checked_out. When hold is placed on book, set state to book[i]_held_for_borrower[k]. When book is returned, if not held_for_borrower set state to available.

*Step 5. Product timing step:*

Time-out functions must be added. If 20 seconds, say, pass between librarian indicating transaction type and providing the input, then the current transaction must be terminated.

*Step 6. Implementation:*

Not asked for in this problem.

90

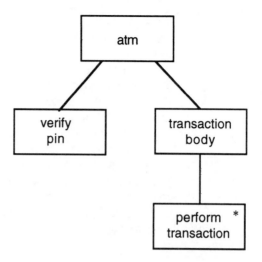

Figure 11.11. JSD structure diagram for automated teller machine.

11.10: *Step 1. Entity action step:*

Entity: customer
    Action:     insert card
    Action:     key in pin
    Action:     choose account
    Action:     choose transaction
    Action:     key in transaction data
    Action:     take card

Entity: atm
    Action:     verify pin
    Action:     perform transaction

*Step 2. Entity structure step:*

The structure diagram for the atm is shown in Figure 11.11, and for the customer in Figure 11.12.

*Step 3. Initial model step:*

The mapping between the model and the real world is shown in Figure 11.13.

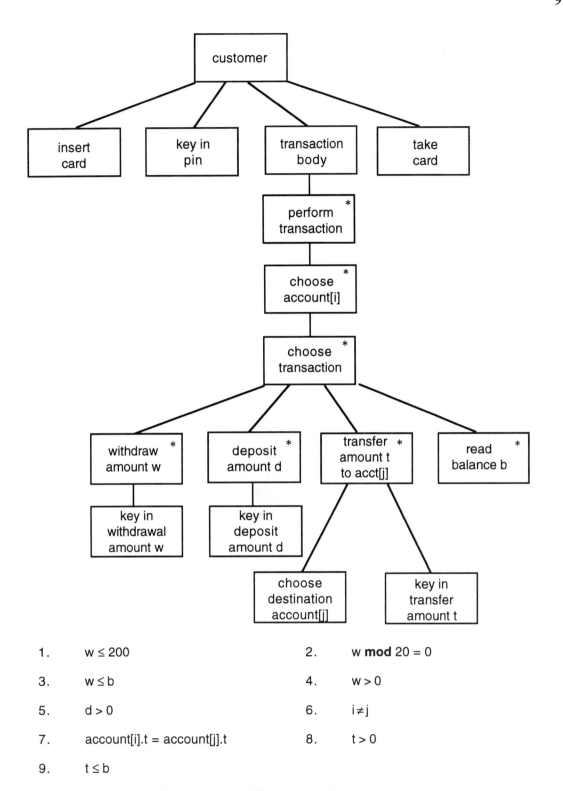

| 1. | $w \leq 200$ | 2. | $w \bmod 20 = 0$ |
|---|---|---|---|
| 3. | $w \leq b$ | 4. | $w > 0$ |
| 5. | $d > 0$ | 6. | $i \neq j$ |
| 7. | $account[i].t = account[j].t$ | 8. | $t > 0$ |
| 9. | $t \leq b$ | | |

Figure 11.12. JSD structure diagram for customer.

92

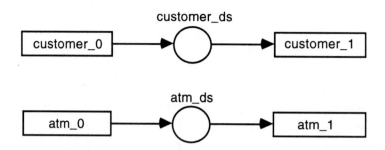

Figure 11.13. Mapping between model and real-world for automated teller machine

The structure text for customer_1 is

```
customer_1 seq
    insert_card;
    key_in_pin;
    transaction_body itr
        perform_transaction itr
            choose_account[i] itr
                choose_transaction sel
                    withdraw_amount seq
                        key_in_withdrawal_amount;
                    withdraw_amount end;
                choose_transaction alt
                    deposit_amount seq
                        key_in_deposit_amount;
                    deposit_amount end;
                choose_transaction alt
                    transfer_amount_to_acct[j] seq
                        choose_destination_account[j];
                        key_in_transfer_amount;
                    transfer_amount_to_acct[j] end;
                choose_transaction alt
                    read_balance;
                choose_transaction end;
            choose_account[i] end;
        perform_transaction end;
    transaction_body end;
    take_card;
customer_1 end;
```

The structure text for atm_1 is

```
atm_1 seq
    read customer_ds;
    verify_pin;
    transaction_body itr
        perform_transaction seq
            read customer_ds;
            perform_transaction;
        perform_transaction end;
```

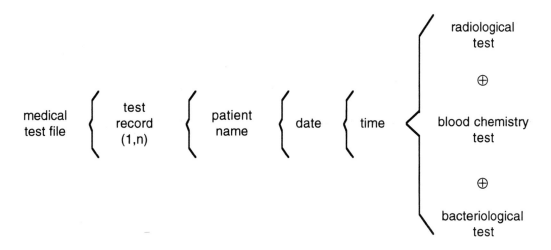

Figure 11.14. Description of medical test file using Warnier's notation.

```
transaction_body end;
atm_1 end;
```

*Step 4.  Function step:*

After the transaction is completed, the ATM must cause the bank records to be updated appropriately.  The ATM must issue the commands to accept the customer's card, and to return it to the customer at the end of the session.

*Step 5.  Product timing step:*

Time-out functions must be added. If 20 seconds, say, pass between successive customer inputs, the current transaction must be terminated, and the card returned to the customer.

*Step 6.  Implementation:*

Not asked for in this problem.

11.11: See Figure 11.14.

11.12: *Step 1.  Determine the actions of the classes:*

The class table is shown in Figure 11.15.

*Step 2.  Design the product in terms of clients of objects:*

The object-client relations in Figure 11.16.

94

| Class | Attributes | Methods |
|---|---|---|
| Book | author<br>book_number<br>borrower_number<br>hold_number<br>subject<br>title | *add_book*<br>*check_out_book*<br>*hold_book*<br>*obtain_information*<br>*remove_book*<br>*return_book* |

Figure 11.15. Object-operations table for automated library system.

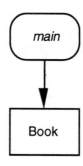

Figure 11.16. Client-object relations for automated library system.

*Step 3. Detailed Design:*

A pseudocode representation of the six modules that access the library database is now given.

```
void add_book (void)
{
    int             book_number;
    string          author, subject, title;

    scan (book_number);
    add_to_database (author, book_number, subject, title);
}

void check_out_book (void)
{
    int             book_number ;
    int             borrower_number;
    BOOK            book;

    scan (borrower_number);
    scan (book_number);
    get_book_record (book_number);

    if book is on hold
    {
        if hold_number is not equal to borrower_number
            display ("Book is on hold for another borrower.");
```

```
    }
    else
        check_out (book_number);
}

void hold_book (void)
{
    int                 book_number ;
    int                 borrower_number;
    BOOK                book;

    get_from_borrower (book_number);
    get_book_record (book_number);

    if book is on hold
        display ("Book is on hold for another borrower.");
    else
    {
        scan (borrower_number);
        hold_for_borrower (book_number, borrower_number);
    }
}


void obtain_information (string request_string)
{

    extract request type from request_string;
    extract author, subject, or title from request_string;
    search for desired book;
    display results of search;
}


void remove_book (void)
{
    int                 book_number ;

    scan (book_number);
    remove_from_database (book_number);
}

void return_book (void)
{
    int                 book_number ;

    scan (book_number);
    return (book_number);
}
```

The next refinement of the detailed design depends critically on how the library is implemented; it is therefore omitted here.

11.13: *Step 1. Determine the actions of the classes:*

| Class | Attributes | Methods |
|---|---|---|
| Account | account_number<br>balance<br>PIN_number | *deposit*<br>*determine_balance*<br>*transfer*<br>*verify_PIN_number*<br>*withdraw* |

Figure 11.17.  Object-operations table for ATM controller.

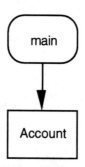

Figure 11.18.  Client-object relations for ATM controller.

The class table is shown in Figure 11.17.

*Step 2.  Design the product in terms of clients of objects:*

The object-client relations in Figure 11.18.

*Step 3: Detailed Design.*

A pseudocode representation of the five methods for class Account is now given.

```
void deposit (void)
{
    int             amount;
    ACCOUNT         account_number;
    DATE            date;

    get_from_customer (amount);
    balance := balance + amount;
    perform_deposit_actions (account_number, amount);
    print_receipt (date, amount, account_number);
}

void determine_balance (void)
{
    int                 balance;

    display (balance);
}
```

```
void transfer (void)
{
    int             amount;
    int             balance;
    ACCOUNT         account_number;
    ACCOUNT         destination_account;
    DATE            date;

    get_from_customer (amount);
    get_from_customer (destination_account);

    if amount > balance
        error_routine ("Amount is greater than current balance.");
    else
    {
        perform_withdraw_actions (account_number, amount);
        perform_deposit_actions (destination_account, amount);
        print_receipt (date, amount, account_number, destination_account);
    }
}

void verify_PIN_number (void)
{
    int                     unverified_number;

    get_from_customer (unverified_number);

    if unverified_number = PIN_number
        return ("okay");
    else
        error_routine ("Invalid PIN number.");
}

void withdraw (void)
{
    int             amount;
    int             balance;
    ACCOUNT         account_number;
    DATE            date;


    get_from_customer (amount);

    if amount mod 20 is not equal to 0
        error_routine ("Amount not in units of $20.");
    else if amount > balance
        error_routine ("Amount is greater than current balance.");
    else if amount > 200
        error_routine ("Amount exceeds $200 limit.");
    else
    {
        perform_withdraw_actions (account_number, amount);
        balance := balance – amount;
        print_receipt (date, amount, account_number, balance);
    }
}
```

98

The detailed design of object Account depends critically on hardware details; it is therefore omitted here.

## TERM PROJECT

11.14: *Step 1.  Determine the actions of the classes:*

The object-operations table is shown in Figure 11.19.

*Step 2.  Design the product in terms of clients of objects:*

The object-client relations are shown in Figure 11.20.

| Class | Attributes | Methods |
|---|---|---|
| Painting_Class | first_name<br>last_name<br>title<br>painting_date<br>medium<br>subject<br>height<br>width | *get_description* |
| Gallery_Class | classification<br>purchase_date<br>sale_date<br>seller_name<br>buyer_name<br>seller_addr<br>buyer_addr<br>alg_price<br>purch_price<br>target_price<br>sell_price | *determine_alg_price* (**virtual**)<br>*get_gallery_information*<br>*add_new_painting*<br>*buy*<br>*bought_report*<br>*read_bought*<br>*write_bought*<br>*add_new_sale*<br>*sell*<br>*sell_report*<br>*read_sold*<br>*write_sold*<br>*fashionability_report* |
| Auction_Class | auction_date<br>auction_price | *read_auction* |
| Masterpiece_Class | | *determine_alg_price* |
| Masterwork_Class | | *determine_alg_price* |
| Other_Class | | *determine_alg_price* |
| Fashionability_Class | first_name<br>last_name<br>coefficient | *get_description*<br>*add_new_fashionability*<br>*read_fashionability*<br>*write_fashionability* |

Figure 11.19. Object-operations table for Osbert Oglesby product.

100

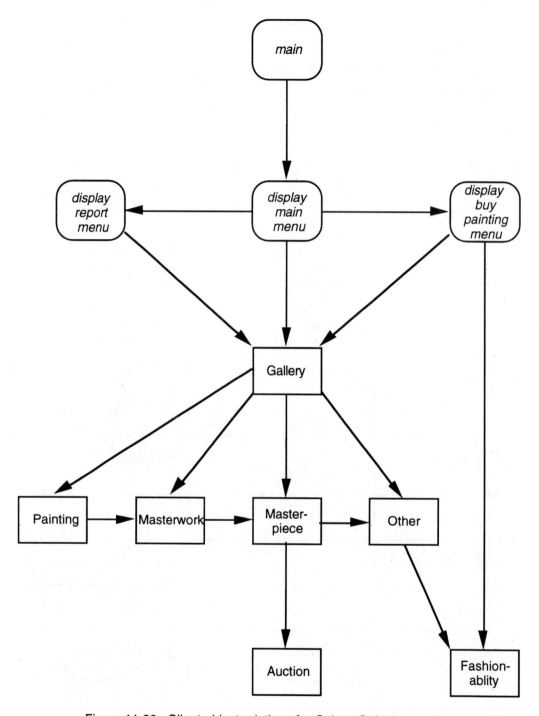

Figure 11.20. Client-object relations for Osbert Oglesby product.

*Step 3. Detailed Design:*

| Module name | *Painting_Class::get_description* |
|---|---|
| Module type | *Method* |
| Input parameters | *None* |
| Output parameters | *None* |
| Error messages | *None* |
| Files accessed | *None* |
| Files changed | *None* |
| Modules called | *None* |
| Narrative | *Retrieves information concerning a painting object (i.e. , attributes* first_name, last_name, title, painting_ date, height, width, medium, subject*)* |

| Module name | *Gallery_Class::get_gallery_information* |
|---|---|
| Module type | *Method* |
| Input parameters | *None* |
| Output parameters | *None* |
| Error messages | *None* |
| Files accessed | *None* |
| Files changed | *None* |
| Modules called | *None* |
| Narrative | *Retrieves additional information concerning a gallery object (i.e. , attributes* purchase_date, seller_name, seller_address, purchase_price, target_ price*)* |

| Module name | *Gallery_Class::add_new_painting* |
|---|---|
| Module type | *Method* |
| Input parameters | *None* |
| Output parameters | *None* |
| Error messages | *None* |
| Files accessed | BOUGHT_FILE, TEMP_BOUGHT_FILE |
| Files changed | BOUGHT_FILE |
| Modules called | *date_compare, read_bought, write_bought* |
| Narrative | *Inserts a new gallery painting in alphabetical order into the* BOUGHT_FILE. *This operation is performed by first copying* BOUGHT_FILE *to* TEMP_ BOUGHT_FILE. *The new painting is then inserted into the correct location while* TEMP_BOUGHT_ FILE *is copied back to* BOUGHT_FILE *record-by-record* |

| Module name | Gallery_Class::buy |
|---|---|
| Module type | Method |
| Input parameters | None |
| Output parameters | None |
| Error messages | None |
| Files accessed | BOUGHT_FILE |
| Files changed | None |
| Modules called | get_description, read_bought, compare_str, determine_alg_price, get_gallery_information, add_new_painting, press_enter |
| Narrative | This method first retrieves information from the user concerning the painting to be purchased. If the painting does not already exist in the gallery, the maximum buying price for the painting is given. The user is then requested to enter additional purchase information before the painting is actually inserted into the gallery via a call to add_new_painting |

| Module name | Gallery_Class::bought_report |
|---|---|
| Module type | Method |
| Input parameters | None |
| Output parameters | None |
| Error messages | None |
| Files accessed | BOUGHT_FILE |
| Files changed | None |
| Modules called | clear_screen, subtract_one_year, read_bought, date_compare, compare_str, press_enter |
| Narrative | Produces bought report by reading BOUGHT_FILE and displaying every gallery object that has been bought over the past year |

| Module name | Gallery_Class::read_bought |
|---|---|
| Module type | Method |
| Input parameters | ifstream |
| Output parameters | None |
| Error messages | None |
| Files accessed | None |
| Files changed | <file pointed to by input stream> |
| Modules called | None |
| Narrative | Reads a gallery object (which has been bought) from the file specified as the input parameter |

| Module name | Gallery_Class::write_bought |
|---|---|
| Module type | Method |
| Input parameters | ofstream |
| Output parameters | None |
| Error messages | None |
| Files accessed | None |
| Files changed | <file pointed to by input stream> |
| Modules called | None |
| Narrative | Writes a gallery object (which has been bought) to the file specified as the input parameter |

| Module name | Gallery_Class::add_new_sale |
|---|---|
| Module type | Method |
| Input parameters | None |
| Output parameters | None |
| Error messages | None |
| Files accessed | SOLD_FILE, TEMP_SOLD_FILE |
| Files changed | SOLD_FILE |
| Modules called | date_compare, read_sold, write_sold |
| Narrative | Inserts a sold painting in alphabetical order into the SOLD_FILE.  This operation is performed by first copying SOLD_FILE to TEMP_SOLD_FILE.  The new painting is then inserted into the correct location as TEMP_SOLD_FILE is copied back to SOLD_FILE record-by-record |

| Module name | Gallery_Class::sell |
|---|---|
| Module type | Method |
| Input parameters | None |
| Output parameters | None |
| Error messages | None |
| Files accessed | SOLD_FILE, BOUGHT_FILE |
| Files changed | None |
| Modules called | read_sold, read_bought, compare_str, add_new_sale, add_artist, press_enter |
| Narrative | This method first retrieves information from the user concerning which gallery painting is to be sold. Then, a check is made to see if the painting exists in the gallery, and if it has already been sold.  If not, the user is then requested to enter the sale information before the painting is actually inserted via a call to add_new_sale.  After recording a valid sale, the artist name is also written to ARTIST_FILE via a call to add_artist |

| Module name | Gallery_Class::sell_report |
|---|---|
| Module type | Method |
| Input parameters | None |
| Output parameters | None |
| Error messages | None |
| Files accessed | SOLD_FILE |
| Files changed | None |
| Modules called | clear_screen, subtract_one_year, read_sold, date_compare, compare_str, press_enter |
| Narrative | Produces sold report by reading SOLD_FILE and displaying every gallery object that has been sold over the past year |

| Module name | Gallery_Class::read_sold |
|---|---|
| Module type | Method |
| Input parameters | ifstream |
| Output parameters | None |
| Error messages | None |
| Files accessed | None |
| Files changed | <file pointed to by input stream> |
| Modules called | None |
| Narrative | Reads a gallery object (which has been sold) from the file specified as the input parameter |

| Module name | Gallery_Class::write_sold |
|---|---|
| Module type | Method |
| Input parameters | ofstream |
| Output parameters | None |
| Error messages | None |
| Files accessed | None |
| Files changed | <file pointed to by input stream> |
| Modules called | None |
| Narrative | Writes a gallery object (which has been sold) to the file specified as the input parameter |

| Module name | Gallery_Class::fashion_report |
|---|---|
| Module type | Method |
| Input parameters | None |
| Output parameters | None |
| Error messages | None |
| Files accessed | ARTIST_FILE, SOLD_FILE |
| Files changed | None |
| Modules called | clear_screen, subtract_one_year, over_target, read_sold, date_compare, compare_str, press_enter |
| Narrative | Produces a fashion report by reading every artist (from ARTIST_FILE) whose paintings have been sold.  For each artist that has every painting (with at least two) from the past year sold over the target price, the artist name and each painting sold over the past year is displayed |

| Module name | Gallery_Class::determine_alg_price |
|---|---|
| Module type | **virtual** method |
| Input parameters | None |
| Output parameters | None |
| Error messages | None |
| Files accessed | None |
| Files changed | None |
| Modules called | None |
| Narrative | This is a virtual method which will be instantiated in the subclasses Masterpiece_Class, Masterwork_Class, and Other_Class |

| Module name | Auction_Class::read_auction |
|---|---|
| Module type | Method |
| Input parameters | ifstream |
| Output parameters | None |
| Error messages | None |
| Files accessed | <file pointed to by input stream> |
| Files changed | None |
| Modules called | None |
| Narrative | Reads an auction object from the file specified as the input parameter |

| Module name | Masterpiece_Class::determine_alg_price |
|---|---|
| Module type | Method |
| Input parameters | None |
| Output parameters | None |
| Error messages | None |
| Files accessed | AUCTION_FILE |
| Files changed | None |
| Modules called | read_auction, compare_str, breakup_date |
| Narrative | Determines the maximum price to be offered for a masterpiece. The AUCTION_FILE is scanned for the most similar work by the artist represented by the masterpiece object. The maximum base price is the purchase price of the most similar record in AUCTION_FILE. The final maximum price is found by adding 8. 5%, compounded annually, to the base price for each year since the auction sale date of the most similar auction record |

| Module name | Masterwork_Class::determine_alg_price |
|---|---|
| Module type | Method |
| Input parameters | None |
| Output parameters | None |
| Error messages | None |
| Files accessed | None |
| Files changed | None |
| Modules called | Masterpiece_Class::determine_alg_price |
| Narrative | Determines the maximum price to be offered for a masterwork. First, the maximum base price is determined as if the masterwork were a master-piece. The final maximum price is the base price multiplied by 0. 25 if the item was painted in the 20th century. For any other century, the base price is multiplied by $(20 - c)/(21 - c)$, where $c$ is the century in which the masterwork was painted |

| Module name | Other_Class::determine_alg_price |
|---|---|
| Module type | Method |
| Input parameters | None |
| Output parameters | None |
| Error messages | None |
| Files accessed | FASHION_FILE |
| Files changed | None |
| Modules called | read_fash, compare_str |
| Narrative | Determines the maximum price to be offered for an "other" piece of work. This operation is performed by first finding the appropriate fashionability coefficient from the FASHION_FILE. The maximum price is then computed as the area of the painting object multiplied by the fashionability coefficient |

| Module name | Fashionability_Class::get_description |
|---|---|
| Module type | Method |
| Input parameters | None |
| Output parameters | None |
| Error messages | None |
| Files accessed | None |
| Files changed | None |
| Modules called | None |
| Narrative | Retrieves fashionability description information (i.e., attributes first_name, last_name, coefficient) |

| Module name | Fashionability_Class::read_fash |
|---|---|
| Module type | Method |
| Input parameters | ifstream |
| Output parameters | None |
| Error messages | None |
| Files accessed | <file pointed to by input stream> |
| Files changed | None |
| Modules called | None |
| Narrative | Reads a fashion object from the file specified as the input parameter |

108

| Module name | Fashionability_Class::write_fash |
|---|---|
| Module type | Method |
| Input parameters | ofstream |
| Output parameters | None |
| Error messages | None |
| Files accessed | None |
| Files changed | <file pointed to by input stream> |
| Modules called | None |
| Narrative | Writes a fashion object to the file specified as the input parameter |

| Module name | Fashionability_Class::add_new_fash |
|---|---|
| Module type | Method |
| Input parameters | None |
| Output parameters | None |
| Error messages | None |
| Files accessed | FASHION_FILE, TEMP_FASHION_FILE |
| Files changed | FASHION_FILE |
| Modules called | get_description, read_fash, write_fash, compare_str |
| Narrative | Inserts a fashion object in alphabetical order (sorted by artist name) into the FASHION_FILE. This operation is performed by first copying FASHION_FILE to TEMP_FASHION_FILE. The new object is then inserted into the correct location while TEMP_FASHION_FILE is copied back to FASHION_FILE record-by-record |

| Module name | main |
|---|---|
| Module type | Function |
| Input parameters | None |
| Output parameters | None |
| Error messages | If invalid current date is entered |
| Files accessed | None |
| Files changed | None |
| Modules called | display_main_menu |
| Narrative | Drives entire product by calling display_main_menu to solicit the user's choice |

| Module name | add_artist |
|---|---|
| Module type | Function |
| Input parameters | string |
| Output parameters | None |
| Error messages | None |
| Files accessed | ARTIST_FILE, TEMP_ARTIST_FILE |
| Files changed | ARTIST_FILE |
| Modules called | compare_str |
| Narrative | Inserts an artist name (represented by the input string) in alphabetical order into the ARTIST_FILE. This operation is performed by first copying ARTIST_FILE to TEMP_ARTIST_FILE. The new information is then inserted into the correct location while TEMP_ARTIST_FILE is copied back to ARTIST_FILE record-by-record |

| Module name | over_target |
|---|---|
| Module type | Function |
| Input parameters | string |
| Output parameters | integer |
| Error messages | None |
| Files accessed | SOLD_FILE |
| Files changed | None |
| Modules called | subtract_one_year, date_compare, compare_str, read_sold |
| Narrative | This function determines if an artist (represented by the input string) has had all of his/her paintings sold over the target price during the past year and that at least two paintings have been sold over the past year. Returns 0 if all paintings (two or more) sold over target, and -1 otherwise |

| Module name | clear_screen |
|---|---|
| Module type | Function |
| Input parameters | None |
| Output parameters | None |
| Error messages | None |
| Files accessed | None |
| Files changed | None |
| Modules called | None |
| Narrative | Clears the screen by emitting a sequence of carriage returns |

110

| Module name | press_enter |
|---|---|
| Module type | Function |
| Input parameters | None |
| Output parameters | None |
| Error messages | None |
| Files accessed | None |
| Files changed | None |
| Modules called | None |
| Narrative | Waits until the user presses the <enter> key |

| Module name | display_main_menu |
|---|---|
| Module type | Function |
| Input parameters | None |
| Output parameters | None |
| Error messages | If an invalid choice is made |
| Files accessed | None |
| Files changed | None |
| Modules called | display_buy_painting_menu, display_report_menu, sell, clear_screen, press_enter |
| Narrative | Displays main menu that drives the product, offering the user the choice of buying a painting, selling a painting, or producing a report; the appropriate method is then called. The user may also choose to quit |

| Module name | display_buy_painting_menu |
|---|---|
| Module type | Function |
| Input parameters | None |
| Output parameters | None |
| Error messages | If an invalid choice is made |
| Files accessed | None |
| Files changed | None |
| Modules called | buy, add_new_fash, clear_screen, press_enter |
| Narrative | Displays buy painting menu, offering the user the choice of buying a masterpiece, masterwork, other, or updating the fashionability coefficients; the appropriate method is then called. The user may also choose to return to the main menu |

| Module name | display_report_menu |
|---|---|
| Module type | Function |
| Input parameters | None |
| Output parameters | None |
| Error messages | If an invalid choice is made |
| Files accessed | None |
| Files changed | None |
| Modules called | bought_report, sell_report, fashion_report, clear_screen, press_enter |
| Narrative | Displays report menu, offering the user the choice of bought paintings report, sold paintings report, and fashion trends report; the appropriate method is then called. The user may also choose to return to the main menu |

| Module name | breakup_date |
|---|---|
| Module type | Function |
| Input parameters | string |
| Output parameters | integer, integer, integer |
| Error messages | None |
| Files accessed | None |
| Files changed | None |
| Modules called | None |
| Narrative | Assuming that the input string represents a valid date of the form mm/dd/yy, this function returns the respective integer components of the date |

| Module name | valid_date |
|---|---|
| Module type | Function |
| Input parameters | string |
| Output parameters | integer |
| Error messages | None |
| Files accessed | None |
| Files changed | None |
| Modules called | breakup_date |
| Narrative | Determines if the input string corresponds to meaningful values for dates of the form mm/dd/yy. Returns 0 if the date is valid, otherwise -1 |

| Module name | date_compare |
|---|---|
| Module type | Function |
| Input parameters | string |
| Output parameters | integer |
| Error messages | None |
| Files accessed | None |
| Files changed | None |
| Modules called | breakup_date |
| Narrative | Determines the temporal order of two dates (represented by two input strings). Returns -1 if first date < second date, 0 if first date = second date, and -1 if first date > second date |

| Module name | subtract_one_year |
|---|---|
| Module type | Function |
| Input parameters | string |
| Output parameters | string |
| Error messages | None |
| Files accessed | None |
| Files changed | None |
| Modules called | breakup_date |
| Narrative | Subtracts 1 year from the input string (represented in the form mm/dd/yy) and stores the result in the output string |

| Module name | remove_q |
|---|---|
| Module type | Function |
| Input parameters | string |
| Output parameters | string |
| Error messages | None |
| Files accessed | None |
| Files changed | None |
| Modules called | None |
| Narrative | Copies the contents of the input string to an output string. The output string will be void of any question marks that may have existed in the input string |

| Module name | compare_str |
|---|---|
| Module type | Function |
| Input parameters | string |
| Output parameters | integer |
| Error messages | None |
| Files accessed | None |
| Files changed | None |
| Modules called | remove_q |
| Narrative | Compares two strings (in the same manner as the C function strcmp) while ignoring any question marks in the strings |

| Module name | stringlower |
|---|---|
| Module type | Function |
| Input parameters | string |
| Output parameters | string |
| Error messages | None |
| Files accessed | None |
| Files changed | None |
| Modules called | None |
| Narrative | Converts string to lowercase, if needed |

# CHAPTER 12

# IMPLEMENTATION PHASE.

This chapter consists of a number of disparate topics connected by the fact that they all apply to the implementation phase. The section on 4GLs is important, if only because many students are unaware that 4GLs exist, let alone their important role in the software industry; students are frequently equally unaware of coding standards (Section 12.5). The misconception that structured programming is **goto**-less programming is difficult to undo unless a historic approach is taken; that is why section 12.3 came to be written.

With regard to programming teams, the fact that the term project is being done in teams tends to make many students particularly interested in Sections 12.6 through 12.9; I always get a plethora of questions about those sections.

With regard to Sections 12.10 through 12.12, the importance of portability cannot be over stressed. At the same time, it is not necessary to cover all the material on portability in detail, especially when teaching undergraduates.

## PROBLEM SOLUTIONS

12.1: Key point: This is essentially a data-processing (DP) product.

C or C++ is a good choice of implementation language, and so is COBOL.

Ada
*Benefits:* truly portable; strongly typed; supports modularity; excellent file handling capabilities; supports abstraction; facilitates implementation of object-oriented design.
*Costs:* unfamiliar to most DP programmers.

BASIC
*Benefits:* quick and easy to use; highly interactive; good string handling; good for DP purposes.
*Costs:* no standard; not modular; slow to execute; not very portable.

C/C++
*Benefits:* powerful constructs; widely available; modular; highly portable; C++ facilitates implementation of object-oriented design and hence reuse.
*Costs:* easy to write dangerous code; low-level file handling; hard to maintain unless carefully written in a style that does not use "fancy" features.

COBOL
*Benefits:* business oriented; largely standardized; widely used and hence many programmers available; widely available; highly portable.
*Costs:* verbose; **perform** statement changes global variables, not parameters; no typing.

FORTRAN
*Benefits:* efficient compilation; efficient to execute; widely implemented.
*Costs:* not business oriented; implicit typing; poor file handling; incompatible language extensions.

Lisp
*Benefits:* interactive.
*Costs:* slow; self-modifying code; not business oriented; hardly known by DP programmers.

Pascal
*Benefits:* easy to use; widely available; block structured.
*Costs:* no separate compilation; incompatible language extensions.

Smalltalk
*Benefits:* strongly object-oriented; highly portable.
*Costs:* not widely used; hardly known by DP programmers.

12.2:   Key point: This is a real-time product.

Ada and C/C++ are good choices of implementation language.

Ada
*Benefits:* truly portable; strongly typed; supports modularity; supports abstraction; facilitates implementation of an object-oriented design; supports concurrent programming; has real-time constructs.
*Costs:* no control over real-time scheduling.

BASIC
*Benefits:* quick and easy to use; highly interactive.
*Costs:* no real-time features; no standard; not modular; slow to execute; not very portable.

C/C++
*Benefits:* powerful constructs; widely available; modular; highly portable; can easily access operating system; C++ facilitates implementation of object-oriented design.
*Costs:* easy to write dangerous code; hard to maintain unless carefully written in a style that does not use "fancy" features; use of operating system calls to achieve real-time constructs reduces portability unless UNIX is used.

COBOL
*Benefits:* largely standardized; widely used and hence many programmers available; widely available; highly portable.
*Costs:* no real-time features; verbose; **perform** statement changes global variables, not parameters; no typing.

FORTRAN
*Benefits:* efficient compilation; efficient to execute; widely implemented.

116

*Costs:* no real-time features; implicit typing; incompatible language extensions.

Lisp
*Benefits:* interactive.
*Costs:* no real-time features; slow; self-modifying code.

Pascal
*Benefits:* easy to use; widely available; block structured.
*Costs:* no real-time features; no separate compilation; incompatible language extensions.

Smalltalk
*Benefits:* strongly object-oriented; highly portable.
*Costs:* no real-time features; not widely used.

12.3: Key point: This product has both real-time and data-processing features.
Answer is therefore a combination of the answers for 12.1 and 12.2. C/C++ is a good choice of language, also Ada.

12.4: Key point: Data processing product that must interface with both a database and bar-code readers.

An appropriate language would be COBOL or C/C++.

Ada
*Benefits:* truly portable; strongly typed; supports modularity; excellent file handling capabilities; supports abstraction; facilitates implementation of object-oriented design; can easily interface with ATM hardware.
*Costs:* unfamiliar to most DP programmers; almost no DBMS interfaces.

BASIC
*Benefits:* quick and easy to use; highly interactive; good string handling; good for DP purposes; some DBMS interfaces.
*Costs:* no standard; not modular; slow to execute; not very portable; BASIC cannot interface with bar-code hardware; assembler subroutines are nonportable.

C/C++
*Benefits:* powerful constructs; widely available; modular; highly portable; can easily interface with bar-code hardware; some DBMS interfaces; C++ facilitates implementation of object-oriented design.
*Costs:* easy to write dangerous code; low-level file handling; hard to maintain unless carefully written in a style that does not use "fancy" features.

COBOL
*Benefits:* business oriented; largely standardized; widely used and hence many programmers available; widely available; highly portable; almost every DBMS has a COBOL interface.
*Costs:* verbose; **perform** statement changes global variables, not parameters; no typing; cannot interface with bar-code hardware; assembler subroutines are nonportable.

FORTRAN
*Benefits:* efficient compilation; efficient to execute; widely implemented.

*Costs:* not business oriented; poor file handling; implicit typing; incompatible language extensions; few DBMS interfaces; cannot interface with bar-code hardware; assembler subroutines are nonportable.

Lisp
*Benefits:* interactive.
*Costs:* slow; self-modifying code; not business oriented; hardly known by DP programmers; virtually no DBMS interfaces; cannot interface directly with bar-code hardware; difficult to interface via (nonportable) assembler subroutines.

Pascal
*Benefits:* easy to use; widely available; block structured.
*Costs:* no separate compilation; incompatible language extensions; standard Pascal cannot interface with bar-code hardware; few DBMS interfaces; assembler subroutines are nonportable.

Smalltalk
*Benefits:* strongly object-oriented; highly portable.
*Costs:* not widely used; hardly known by DP programmers; few DBMS interfaces; difficult to interface via (nonportable) assembler subroutines.

12.5:   Key point: This is also a data processing (DP) product. The answer is therefore the same as for Problem 12.1.

12.6:   From Figure 12.2 of *Classical and Object-Oriented Software Engineering*, all three constructs have one entry and one exit. Blocks are therefore linear sections of code. Since labels are forbidden, branches into and out of a block are forbidden. Each block thus has a first statement and a last statement, and the order of execution cannot be changed. Each block will therefore have only one entry and one exit.

12.8:   There should be no difference at all because of the possibility that the organization will expand or be sold to someone else. Also, there is no guarantee that at maintenance time the one-person software developer will recall every detail of every module he or she has written. Finally, lack of an independent SQA function in a one-person environment means that particular care has to be taken to reduce faults, and adhering to standards is one such way.

12.9:   In theory there should be no difference whatsoever; software should always be built to the highest possible standards. In practice, however, a company that builds intensive care units will usually take greater care to ensure that their software is correct because human lives are at stake. (It is sad but true that, for many companies, the real reason they will take greater care is because of the risk of being sued should the intensive care unit software malfunction.) In order to achieve higher quality software, coding standards are likely to be more detailed and more rigorously enforced.

12.10:  *Payroll project:* Chief programmer team. This is a standard application area, so an experienced chief programmer with a team of two reasonably competent programmers should do a credible job.
        *Avionics software:* As in Figure 12.13 of *Classical and Object-Oriented Software Engineering*. The hardness of the problem requires the synergistic effect of group interaction at each level, but the scale of the problem and the need for strict controls (military project) requires a hierarchy. Regulatory and budgetary considerations require nontechnical management.

12.11: It is true that almost all the problems that inhibit democratic teams are absent. Nevertheless, a democratic team consists of a group working towards a common goal. Attempts to implement democratic teams will therefore fail unless all the employees can be motivated to work in this fashion.

12.12: Use a standard high-level language, a popular operating system; meticulously maintain documentation; data files should be as unstructured as possible, and no database management tool of any kind should be used; the sort utility that comes with the operating system should not be used.

12.13: Use a standard high-level language, a popular operating system; meticulously maintain documentation; each hardware component should have its own separate driver; design should allow for different cataloguing schemes (Dewey, Library of Congress, and so on) and different bar-codes; use object-oriented techniques; indexing techniques should be generic, and not specific to the operating system; hardware-dependent components should be isolated.

12.14: Use a standard high-level language, a popular operating system; meticulously maintain documentation; product must be designed using levels of abstraction, with hardware dependence and database dependence restricted to the lowest level modules, and carefully documented; generalized accounting practices should be followed, rather than those of one specific bank; product should be parametrized to be able to handle different numbers of accounts.

12.15: Design the module using pseudocode, and include the detailed design statements as comments in the code; document the modules profusely, especially prologue and inline comments; make the assumption (all too frequently valid) that the professional who will do the porting to a new machine will be unfamiliar with the assembler you are using.

12.16: Write a precompiler that will transform the nonstandard calls into standard syntax or use an editor macro. (Writing FORTRAN subroutines with the names of the nonstandard input/output routines and making those subroutines call the standard FORTRAN input/output routines does not work, because input/output routines need to have variable numbers of arguments. This is not supported by FORTRAN.)

12.17: Use boundary value analysis. As in the solution to Problem 5.15, input characters can be categorized as NEWLINE (new line character), BLANK (blank character), EOF (end of file character), or other (any other characters).

1. *Test Case:* Empty file.
   *Expected Outcome:* NEWLINE
2. *Test Case:* File consists of BLANK only.
   *Expected Outcome:* NEWLINE
3. *Test Case:* File consists of NEWLINE only.
   *Expected Outcome:* NEWLINE
4. *Test Case:* Words separated by a single BLANK or NEWLINE, and with all words of length less than MAXPOS characters.
   *Expected Outcome:* Outputs the text correctly.
5. *Test Case:* At least one word of length MAXPOS characters.
   *Expected Outcome:* The word is displayed on a line by itself.
6. *Test Case:* At least one word of length greater than MAXPOS characters.
   *Expected Outcome:* Error, word too long.

7.  *Test Case:* More than one BLANK and a single NEWLINE following text.
    *Expected Outcome:* All blanks are ignored and a single NEWLINE is appended to text.
8.  *Test Case:* More than one BLANK and a single NEWLINE preceding text.
    *Expected Outcome:* BLANK is ignored, a single NEWLINE is printed and then text is processed.
9.  *Test Case:* Words separated by more than one BLANK and more than one NEWLINE.
    *Expected Outcome:* Each BLANK is ignored and each word may be printed on a separate line.
10. *Test Case:* Last word followed by no BLANK and no NEWLINE.
    *Expected Outcome:* Text is printed with a NEWLINE appended to last word.

12.18: Refer to Figures 5.2 and 5.3 of this Instructor's Manual. In the test cases for statement coverage, c stands for a single character which is not BLANK or NEWLINE, c+ stands for one or more such characters. The item(s) in parentheses are the transitions tested by this test case.

1.  *Test Case:* BLANK (T1)
    *Expected Output:* NEWLINE
2.  *Test Case:* Empty file (T2)
    *Expected Output:* NEWLINE
3.  *Test Case:* NEWLINE (T1)
    *Expected Output:* NEWLINE
4.  *Test Case:* c (T3, T5)
    *Expected Output:* c NEWLINE
5.  *Test Case:* c BLANK (T4, T9)
    *Expected Output:* c NEWLINE
6.  *Test Case:* c c (T6)
    *Expected Output:* c c NEWLINE
7.  *Test Case:* c+, length > MAXPOS (T7)
    *Expected Output:* Error, word too long
8.  *Test Case:* c+ BLANK BLANK (T8)
    *Expected Output:* c+ NEWLINE
9.  *Test Case:* c+ BLANK (T9)
    *Expected Output:* c+ NEWLINE
10. *Test Case:* c+ BLANK c, combined length ≤ MAXPOS (T10, T12)
    *Expected Output:* c+ BLANK c NEWLINE
11. *Test Case:* c+ BLANK c BLANK, combined length ≤ MAXPOS (T11)
    *Expected Output:* c+ BLANK c NEWLINE
12. *Test Case:* c+ BLANK c BLANK, combined length > MAXPOS (T11)
    *Expected Output:* c+ NEWLINE c NEWLINE
13. *Test Case:* c+ BLANK c, combined length > MAXPOS (T12)
    *Expected Output:* c+ NEWLINE c NEWLINE
14. *Test Case:* c+ BLANK c c (T13)
    *Expected Output:* c+ BLANK c BLANK c c NEWLINE
15. *Test Case:* c+ BLANK c+, length of second c+ > MAXPOS (T14)
    *Expected Output:* Error, word too long

120

12.19: As a consequence of the tree-like structure of the program (other than the overall loop), branch-coverage test cases for this problem are identical to statement-coverage test cases (Problem 12.18).

12.20: Variable state is defined at the beginning of the program, and used by the **while** statement. Every test case uses this path. In addition, the value of state is changed by every transition except T1, T6, T8, and T13, after which control returns to the **while** statement which then uses the value. Variable current_char is defined by function get_character and is used by every transition, specifically by the **switch** (current_char) statements. Thus the define-use test-cases corresponding to variables state and current_char correspond exactly to the test cases of Problem 12.18.

Turning now to variable line_length, it is defined just before the **while** loop, and in transitions T4, T11, and T12. It is used in transitions T11 and T12. The test cases for this are as follows:

Defined in T4:
    Used in T11:        Cases 10, 11 above
    Used in T12:        Cases 12, 13 above

Defined in T11:
    Used in T11:        *Test Case:* c+ BLANK c BLANK c BLANK
                      *Expected Output:* c+ BLANK c BLANK c NEWLINE
    Used in T12:        *Test Case:* c+ BLANK c BLANK c
                      *Expected Output:* c+ BLANK c BLANK c NEWLINE

Defined in T12:        Program terminates

As for variable word, it is defined just before the **while** loop, and in transitions T3, T4, T6, T10, T11, and T13. It is used in the same 6 transitions, and also in T14.

Defined in T3:        Covered by previous cases

Defined in T4:        Covered by previous cases

Defined in T6:
    Used in T3:        Impossible
    Used in T4:        *Test Case:* c c BLANK
                      *Expected Output:* c c NEWLINE
    Used in T6:        *Test Case:* c c c
                      *Expected Output:* c c c NEWLINE
    Used in T10:        *Test Case:* c c BLANK c
                      *Expected Output:* c c BLANK c NEWLINE
    Used in T11:        *Test Case:* c c BLANK c BLANK
                      *Expected Output:* c c BLANK c NEWLINE
    Used in T13:        *Test Case:* c c BLANK c c
                      *Expected Output:* c c BLANK c c NEWLINE
    Used in T14:        *Test Case:* c c BLANK c c+, length > MAXPOS
                      *Expected Output:* Error, word too long

Defined in T10:

| | |
|---|---|
| Used in T3, T4, T6: | Impossible |
| Used in T10: | *Test Case:* c+ BLANK c BLANK c |
| | *Expected Output:* c+ BLANK c BLANK c NEWLINE |
| Used in T11: | *Test Case:* c+ BLANK c BLANK |
| | *Expected Output:* c+ BLANK c NEWLINE |
| Used in T13: | *Test Case:* c+ BLANK c c |
| | *Expected Output:* c+ BLANK c c NEWLINE |
| Used in T14: | *Test Case:* c+ BLANK c+, length > MAXPOS |
| | *Expected Output:* Error, word too long |

Defined in T11:

| | |
|---|---|
| Used in T3, T4, T6: | Impossible |
| Used in T10: | *Test Case:* c+ BLANK c BLANK c |
| | *Expected Output:* c+ BLANK c BLANK c NEWLINE |
| Used in T11: | *Test Case:* c+ BLANK c BLANK c BLANK |
| | *Expected Output:* c+ BLANK c BLANK c NEWLINE |
| Used in T13: | *Test Case:* c+ BLANK c BLANK c c |
| | *Expected Output:* c+ BLANK c BLANK c c NEWLINE |
| Used in T14: | *Test Case:* c+ BLANK c BLANK c+, length > MAXPOS |
| | *Expected Output:* Error, word too long |

Defined in T13:

| | |
|---|---|
| Used in T3, T4, T6: | Impossible |
| Used in T10: | *Test Case:* c+ BLANK c c BLANK c |
| | *Expected Output:* c+ BLANK c c BLANK c NEWLINE |
| Used in T11: | *Test Case:* c+ BLANK c c BLANK |
| | *Expected Output:* c+ BLANK c c NEWLINE |
| Used in T13: | *Test Case:* c+ BLANK c c c |
| | *Expected Output:* c+ BLANK c c c NEWLINE |
| Used in T14: | *Test Case:* c+ BLANK c+, length > MAXPOS |
| | *Expected Output:* Error, word too long |

12.21: Again, the tree-like structure of the design assures that the same test cases as those of Problem 12.18 are obtained. As an additional check, the instructor may care to examine each of the 18 paths in the flowchart displayed in Figure 5.3, and assure himself or herself that all paths are tested by the set of 15 test cases.

12.22: L = {start, **while** statement, **switch** statements, all **case** statements, **default** statement, all **if** statements, all **else** statements, all **break** statements, end}

Referring to the flowchart of Figure 5.3, the paths connecting elements of L are precisely the branch coverage test cases of Problem 12.19 (and hence Problem 12.18).

12.23: The flowchart for two of the four procedures is shown in Figure 5.3. From the flowchart $e = 4 + 31$, $n = 3 + 15$, $c = 2$, so cyclomatic number $M = 35 - 18 + 2 \times 2 = 21$.

12.24: Distinct operators are

**for** ( ... )      =           ;           <           ++           +           [ ]

so $n_1 = 7$

Distinct operands are

| j | 0 | total | value |
|---|---|-------|-------|

so $n_2 = 4$

$N_1 = 8$
$N_2 = 9$

12.25: Structure editor — A considerable amount of time is spent writing and modifying code.

Source level debugger — A considerable amount of time is also spent debugging.

Operating system front end — One person will be writing all parts of all products, and will therefore be helped by a suitably tailored operating system.

Online interface checker — Although most modules will be familiar, this feature helps to reduce errors.

Online documentation — Even though one person can use manuals, updating of online documentation is easier. Also, online documentation is always easy to find, and generally well indexed.

12.26: Structure editor — A considerable amount of time is still spent writing and modifying code.

Online interface checker — Different individuals and teams will write various modules, so this feature is essential to reduce faults.

Source level debugger — A considerable amount of time is still spent debugging.

Online documentation — Multiple copies of manuals are expensive to produce and murderous to update.

Operating system front end — A suitably tailored operating system can aid productivity; at the very least, a front-end can simplify the edit–compile–link–execute cycle.

## TERM PROJECT

12.27: Black box test cases for the OOAD product.

Using boundary value analysis and functional analysis, the following black box test cases have been created for the OOAD product.

*Boundary value analysis:*

Painting data:

Equivalence classes for first name and last name
| | | |
|---|---|---|
| 1. | First character not alphabetic | Error |
| 2. | < 1 character | Error |
| 3. | 1 character | Acceptable |
| 4. | Between 1 and 21 characters | Acceptable |
| 5. | 21 characters | Acceptable |
| 6. | > 21 characters | Acceptable (truncated to 21 characters) |

Equivalence classes for title
| | | |
|---|---|---|
| 1. | < 1 character | Error |
| 2. | 1 character | Acceptable |
| 3. | Between 1 and 41 characters | Acceptable |
| 4. | 41 characters | Acceptable |
| 5. | > 41 characters | Acceptable (truncated to 41 characters) |

Equivalence classes for painting date
| | | |
|---|---|---|
| 1. | Valid date of the form mm/dd/yy | Acceptable |
| 2. | Missing "/" in proper location | Error |
| 3. | Missing leading zero (e.g., 6/16/94 instead of 06/16/94) | Error |
| 4. | Month component < 1 | Error |
| 5. | Month component > 12 | Error |
| 6. | Day component < 1 | Error |
| 7. | Day component > 31 | Error |
| 8. | Year component < 0 | Error |
| 9. | Year component > 99 | Error |

(Additional tests could be made to check that the number of days is valid for the corresponding month; for example, the month of February should not have 31 days).

Equivalence classes for medium
| | | |
|---|---|---|
| 1. | "oil" | Acceptable |
| 2. | "watercolor" | Acceptable |
| 3. | "other" | Acceptable |
| 4. | Any other string | Error (invalid value) |

Equivalence classes for subject
| | | |
|---|---|---|
| 1. | "portrait" | Acceptable |
| 2. | "still-life" | Acceptable |
| 3. | "landscape" | Acceptable |
| 4. | "other" | Acceptable |
| 5. | Any other string | Error (invalid value) |

Equivalence classes for height and width
| | | |
|---|---|---|
| 1. | < 0.00 | Error |
| 2. | 0.00 | Error |
| 3. | 0.01 | Acceptable |

| | | |
|---|---|---|
| 4. | 0.01 and 9999.99 | Acceptable |
| 5. | 10000.00 | Error |
| 6. | > 10000.00 | Error |
| 7. | Characters instead of integers | Error (not a number) |

Gallery data:

(Attributes classification, purchase date, sale date, algorithm price, and target price are determined by the system, and are not entered by the user.)

Equivalence classes for seller name and buyer name

| | | |
|---|---|---|
| 1. | First character not alphabetic | Error |
| 2. | < 1 character | Error |
| 3. | 1 character | Acceptable |
| 4. | Between 1 and 21 characters | Acceptable |
| 5. | 21 characters | Acceptable |
| 6. | > 21 characters | Acceptable (truncated to 21 characters) |

Equivalence classes for seller address and buyer address

| | | |
|---|---|---|
| 1. | < 1 character | Error |
| 2. | 1 character | Acceptable |
| 3. | Between 1 and 25 characters | Acceptable |
| 4. | 25 characters | Acceptable |
| 5. | > 25 characters | Acceptable (truncated to 25 characters) |

Equivalence classes for purchase price and selling price

| | | |
|---|---|---|
| 1. | < 0.00 | Error |
| 2. | 0.00 | Acceptable |
| 3. | 0.01 | Acceptable |
| 4. | Between 0.01 and 999.99 | Acceptable |
| 5. | 1000.00 | Error |
| 6. | > 1000.00 | Error |
| 7. | Characters instead of integers | Error (not a number) |

Fashionability data:

Equivalence classes for first name and last name

| | | |
|---|---|---|
| 1. | First character not alphabetic | Error |
| 2. | < 1 character | Error |
| 3. | 1 character | Acceptable |
| 4. | Between 1 and 21 characters | Acceptable |
| 5. | 21 characters | Acceptable |
| 6. | > 21 characters | Acceptable (truncated to 21 characters) |

Equivalence classes for coefficient

| | | |
|---|---|---|
| 1. | < 0.00 | Error |
| 2. | 0.00 | Error |
| 3. | 0.01 | Acceptable |
| 4. | 0.01 and 9999.99 | Acceptable |
| 5. | 10000.00 | Error |
| 6. | > 10000.00 | Error |
| 7. | Characters instead of integers | Error (not a number) |

*Functional Analysis:*

The functions outlined in the specifications document are used to create test cases.

1. Buy a masterpiece where the artist cannot be found in the auction records.
2. Buy a masterpiece where the artist can be found in the auction records.
3. Buy a masterwork where the artist cannot be found in the auction records.
4. Buy a masterwork where the artist can be found in the auction records.
5. Update the fashionability coefficients of several artists.
6. Buy another type of painting where the artist cannot be found in the fashion records.
7. Buy another type of painting where the artist can be found in the fashion records.
8. Buy a painting where the purchase price is less than the algorithm suggested price.
9. Buy a painting where the purchase price is equal to the algorithm suggested price.
10. Buy a painting where the purchase price is greater than the algorithm suggested price.
11. Sell a painting where the selling price is less than the target price.
12. Sell a painting where the selling price is equal to the target price.
13. Sell a painting where the selling price is greater than the target price.
14. For one or more artists, sell at least two paintings where every painting is sold over the target price (to be used in test case 17).
15. Display report of bought paintings.
16. Display report of sold paintings.
17. Display report of fashion trends.

In addition to these direct tests, it is necessary to perform the following additional tests:

18. Attempt to buy a painting that is already in the gallery.
19. Attempt to sell a painting that does not exist in the gallery.
20. Attempt to sell a painting that has already been sold.

# CHAPTER 13

# IMPLEMENTATION AND INTEGRATION PHASE

Too many software organizations still have a separate implementation phase and a separate integration phase. The resulting lack of fault isolation means that resources are needlessly squandered on unnecessary testing. When I teach this chapter, I stress the financial savings that accrue when implementation and integration are combined into one phase.

## PROBLEM SOLUTIONS

13.1:  Logic modules incorporate the decision-making control flow of the product. A typical example is module main in a large product. The operational modules perform the actual operations of the product, such as test_parity_of_word or add_atomic_weights.

13.2:  Use sandwich implementation and integration to ensure that operational modules are implemented and integrated bottom-up. As a result, these modules are tested using drivers, not defensively programmed modules.

13.3:  Product testing is essentially a dress rehearsal for the acceptance test. As a consequence, the aim of product testing is to be as close as possible to acceptance testing in every way. The major difference is that product testing is performed by the developers, acceptance testing by the client. Also, acceptance testing should be performed as far as possible on actual data, not test data, whereas this may not be possible for product testing.

13.4:  The SQA group manages the implementation and integration phase. In addition, the group is responsible for quality assurance aspects, as with every other phase.

13.5:  Key points: To stay competitive, automation is needed in the software development process. CASE tools can lead to better quality products being delivered sooner, and with fewer faults. Even in the one-person environment, CASE provides management tools such as version control and supplies the management information needed for financial control.

13.6:  Three types of environments should be mentioned and the advantages of each pointed out. First, a graphical upperCASE environment that incorporates a data dictionary, design tool, consistency checker, and screen and report generators. This will ensure that better specification documents are produced, the design will be consistent with the specifications, and screens and reports can quickly be generated automatically. Second, a coding environment based on a structure editor and incorporating an online interface checker, operating system front end, interactive source level debugger, and online documentation will result in better quality code being quickly produced. Third, a configuration management environment will give control over all versions of all modules during the integration and subsequent phases, especially maintenance.

A language-centered environment is meaningful in this context, as does a toolkit environment. A method-based environment makes sense if a specific method is currently being used. But if not, now would not be an optimal time to introduce a whole new way of developing software, so a method-based environment should not be pushed—yet. The situation regarding an integrated environment is similar.

13.7: Take the bequest, and purchase a business-oriented environment together with the hardware necessary to run it. Then, either develop software for larger machines making use of your competitive advantage of having a business-oriented environment, or use the bequest to develop software on the larger machine to be run on a personal computer and then port the finished product to a personal computer. Alternatively, combine the two approaches and develop software that could be run either on larger or smaller machines.

13.8: Key point: If students have not been trained using CASE tools, then they have been inadequately trained. So buy as much as the limited software budget allows even if this means that only one or two copies of each tool can be purchased, and ensure that every student gets some exposure to every CASE tool.

13.9: The difference between introducing CASE tools in a city administration and in a commercial organization is that cities are generally short of money and are loathe to spend available funds on "high tech." The real problem is to convince the city council (and ultimately, the taxpayers) that investing in CASE tools will save money in the long run. In the experience of the author, unless the mayor is personally committed to CASE, little or nothing will be done.

## TERM PROJECT

13.10: The solution presented below is what might be expected from a team of average-to-good students. That is to say, the product tests successfully against most (but not all) of the black box test cases of Problem 12.27. If the input routines were adequate for all test cases, and robust as well, then the product would be larger than what many instructors would consider to be reasonable.

The product will run on a computer terminal—no use is made of any nonstandard screen capabilities.

In order to run this product, it is necessary to set up a file of auction data named auction.dat. A specimen file appears in Figure 13.1. The underscores are required in the various strings; spaces are forbidden in input strings.

To aid in understanding the term project, an alphabetical list of the methods and functions in the implementation appears in Figure 13.2.

```
Leonardo da_Vinci Ceiling_Painting 1530 482.5 530.9 oil other 11/20/70 43.4
Rembrandt van_Rijn The_Day_Watch 1650 90.7 41.3 oil still_life 03/16/63 13.6
Frans Hals The_Manic-Depressive_Cavalier 1616 103.3 61.7 oil portrait 04/22/86 23.4
Edouard Manet Portrait_of_Claude_Monet 1871 43.6 51.4 watercolor portrait 01/04/52 1.1
Claude Monet Portrait_of_Edouard_Manet 1871 43.6 51.4 watercolor portrait 01/04/52 1.1
Vintcent van_Gogh Irises,_Sunflowers,_Wheat 1888 174.2 89.9 oil landscape 10/31/84 6.1
Georges Seurat Lots_of_Tiny_Colored_Dots 1889 206.1 307.6 oil landscape 05/29/90 20.4
```

Figure 13.1. Specimen auction.dat file.

Methods:

*Auction_Class::read_auction* .......... 152
*Fashionability_Class::add_new_fash* .......... 157
*Fashionability_Class::get_description* .......... 156
*Fashionability_Class::read_fash* .......... 156
*Fashionability_Class::write_fash* .......... 157
*Gallery_Class::add_new_painting* .......... 135
*Gallery_Class::add_new_sale* .......... 142
*Gallery_Class::bought_report* .......... 139
*Gallery_Class::buy* .......... 137
*Gallery_Class::fashion_report* .......... 149
*Gallery_Class::get_gallery_information* .......... 135
*Gallery_Class::read_bought* .......... 141
*Gallery_Class::read_sold* .......... 149
*Gallery_Class::sell* .......... 144
*Gallery_Class::sell_report* .......... 147
*Gallery_Class::write_bought* .......... 141
*Gallery_Class::write_sold* .......... 149
*Masterpiece_Class::determine_alg_price* .......... 152
*Masterwork_Class::determine_alg_price* .......... 154
*Other_Class::determine_alg_price* .......... 155
*Painting_Class::get_description* .......... 133

Functions:

*add_artist* .......... 159
*breakup_date* .......... 167
*clear_screen* .......... 163
*compare_str* .......... 171
*date_compare* .......... 168
*display_buy_painting_menu* .......... 165
*display_main_menu* .......... 164
*display_report_menu* .......... 166
*main* .......... 159
*over_target* .......... 161
*press_enter* .......... 163
*remove_q* .......... 170
*stringlower* .......... 171
*subtract_one_year* .......... 169
*valid_date* .......... 168

Figure 13.2. Alphabetical list of methods and functions in implementation of Osbert Oglesby product.

```
#include  <stdio.h>
#include  <string.h>
#include  <stdlib.h>
#include  <iostream.h>
#include  <fstream.h>
#include  <ctype.h>

//
// Boolean values
//
#define FALSE   0
#define TRUE    1

//
// constants
//
#define   TARGET_MARKUP        2.15
#define   ANNUAL_INTEREST      1.085

//
// field lengths
//
#define   DATE_LENGTH             9
#define   NAME_LENGTH             21
#define   ADDR_LENGTH             25
#define   CLASSIFICATION_LENGTH   11
#define   TITLE_LENGTH            41
#define   MED_SUB_LENGTH          10

//
// lengths of strings
//
typedef   char   DATE_TYPE[DATE_LENGTH + 1];
typedef   char   NAME_TYPE[NAME_LENGTH + 1];
typedef   char   ADDR_TYPE[ADDR_LENGTH + 1];
typedef   char   CLASSIFICATION_TYPE[CLASSIFICATION_LENGTH + 1];
typedef   char   TITLE_TYPE[TITLE_LENGTH + 1];
typedef   char   MED_SUB_TYPE[MED_SUB_LENGTH + 1];

//
// functions declared outside of any object
//
void    add_artist (char *fn, char *ln);
int     over_target (char *fn, char *ln);
void    clear_screen (void);
void    press_enter (void);
void    display_main_menu (void);
void    display_buy_painting_menu (void);
void    display_report_menu (void);
void    breakup_date (char *date, int &year, int &month, int &day);
int     valid_date (char *date);
int     date_compare (char *date1, char *date2);
void    subtract_one_year (char *date1, char *date2);
void    remove_q (char *s, char *t);
int     compare_str (char *s, char *t);
```

```
void    stringlower (char *s);

//
// global variable
//
DATE_TYPE               current_date;       // contains today's date

//-----------------------------------------------------------------------------------------

class Painting_Class
{
protected:

    //
    // class data members
    //
    NAME_TYPE           first_name;         // first name of artist
    NAME_TYPE           last_name;          // last name of artist
    TITLE_TYPE          title;              // title of painting
    DATE_TYPE           painting_date;      // date painting was created
    MED_SUB_TYPE        medium;             // medium of painting
    MED_SUB_TYPE        subject;            // subject of painting
    float               height;             // height of painting (in cm)
    float               width;              // width of painting (in cm)

public:

    //
    // data member access functions
    //
    char*   get_first_name ()                       { return first_name; }
    char*   get_last_name ()                        { return last_name; }
    char*   get_title ()                            { return title; }
    char*   get_paint_date ()                       { return painting_date; }
    char*   get_medium ()                           { return medium; }
    char*   get_subject ()                          { return subject; }
    float   get_height ()                           { return height; }
    float   get_width ()                            { return width; }

    //
    // class member function
    //
    void    get_description (void);

}; // class Painting_Class

//-----------------------------------------------------------------------------------------

class Gallery_Class: public Painting_Class
{
protected:

    //
    // class data members
```

```
//
CLASSIFICATION_TYPE   classification;      // gallery classification type
DATE_TYPE             purchase_date;       // date painting was purchased
DATE_TYPE             sale_date;           // date painting was sold
NAME_TYPE             seller_name;         // full name of seller
NAME_TYPE             buyer_name;          // full name of painting buyer
ADDR_TYPE             seller_addr;         // address of seller
ADDR_TYPE             buyer_addr;          // address of buyer
float                 alg_price;           // price determined by algorithm
float                 purchase_price;      // actual purchase price
float                 target_price;        // target selling price
float                 sell_price;          // actual selling price

public:

    //
    // data member access functions
    //
    char*  get_classification ()           { return classification; }
    char*  get_purchase_date ()            { return purchase_date; }
    char*  get_sale_date ()                { return sale_date; }
    char*  get_seller_name ()              { return seller_name; }
    char*  get_buyer_name ()               { return buyer_name; }
    char*  get_seller_addr ()              { return seller_addr; }
    char*  get_buyer_addr ()               { return buyer_addr; }
    float  get_alg_price ()                { return alg_price; }
    float  get_purchase_price ()           { return purchase_price; }
    float  get_target_price ()             { return target_price; }
    float  get_sell_price ()               { return sell_price; }

    //
    // class member functions
    //
    void   get_gallery_information (void);
    void   add_new_painting (void);
    void   buy (void);
    void   bought_report (void);
    void   read_bought (ifstream& file_name);
    void   write_bought (ofstream& file_name);
    void   add_new_sale (void);
    void   sell (void);
    void   sell_report (void);
    void   read_sold (ifstream& file_name);
    void   write_sold (ofstream& file_name);
    void   fashion_report (void);

    //
    // virtual method
    //
    virtual void   determine_alg_price (void) {}

}; // class Gallery_Class

class Auction_Class: public Painting_Class
{
```

132

```
    protected:

        //
        // class data members
        //
        DATE_TYPE           auction_date;        // date painting sold at auction
        float               auction_price;       // auction price of painting

    public:

        //
        // data member access functions
        //
        char*   get_auction_date ()                  { return auction_date; }
        float   get_auction_price ()                 { return auction_price; }

        //
        // class member function
        //
        void    read_auction (ifstream& file_name);

}; // class Auction_Class

class Masterpiece_Class: public Gallery_Class
{
public:

        Masterpiece_Class ()                         { strcpy (classification, "Masterpiece"); }

        //
        // class member function
        //
        void    determine_alg_price (void);

}; // class Masterpiece_Class

//-----------------------------------------------------------------------------------------------------

//
// class Masterwork_Class:
//
class Masterwork_Class: public Masterpiece_Class
{
public:

        Masterwork_Class ()                          { strcpy (classification, "Masterwork"); }

        //
        // class member function
        //
        void    determine_alg_price (void);

}; // class Masterwork_Class

//-----------------------------------------------------------------------------------------------------
```

```
class Other_Class: public Gallery_Class
{
public:

    Other_Class ()                                    { strcpy (classification, "Other"); }

    //
    // class member function
    //
    void    determine_alg_price (void);

}; // class Other_Class
```

//-------------------------------------------------------------------------------------------------

```
class Fashionability_Class
{
protected:

    //
    // class data members
    //
    NAME_TYPE          first_name;         // first name of artist
    NAME_TYPE          last_name;          // last name of artist
    float              coefficient;        // fashionability coefficient

public:

    //
    // data member access functions
    //
    char*   get_first_name ()              { return first_name; }
    char*   get_last_name ()               { return last_name; }
    float   get_coefficient ()             { return coefficient; }

    //
    // class member functions
    //
    void    get_description (void);
    void    add_new_fash (void);
    void    read_fash (ifstream& file_name);
    void    write_fash (ofstream& file_name);

}; // class Fashionability_Class
```

//-------------------------------------------------------------------------------------------------

```
void Painting_Class::get_description (void)
//
// retrieves painting description information
//
{
    int                valid;
```

```
clear_screen ();

cout << "Please enter the following information about the painting:\n\n";

cout << "Note: - Use an underscore in place of any spaces.\n";
cout << "      - Do not leave any request blank.\n\n\n";

cout << endl << endl;

cout << "Enter the FIRST name of the artist (append ? if uncertain): ";
cin >> first_name;

cout << "Enter the LAST name of the artist (append ? if uncertain): ";
cin >> last_name;

cout << "Enter the TITLE of the painting (append ? if uncertain): ";
cin >> title;

cout << "Enter the DATE the painting was created (yyyy) (append ? if uncertain): ";
cin >> painting_date;

cout << "Enter the HEIGHT of the painting (in centimeters): ";
cin >> height;

cout << "Enter the WIDTH of the painting (in centimeters): ";
cin >> width;

//
// retrieves and validates a value for medium
//
valid = FALSE;
while (!valid)
{
    cout << "Enter the MEDIUM of the painting (oil, watercolor, other): ";
    cin >> medium;
    stringlower (medium);

    if ((strcmp (medium, "oil") == 0) || (strcmp (medium, "watercolor") == 0)
            || (strcmp (medium, "other") == 0))
        valid = TRUE;
    else
    {
        cout << endl << "Invalid response!" << endl;
        cout << "Please enter one of the following:";
        cout << " oil, watercolor, other" << endl << endl;
    }
}

//
// retrieves and validates a value for subject
//
valid = FALSE;
while (!valid)
{
    cout << "Enter the SUBJECT of the painting (portrait, landscape, still-life, other): ";
    cin >> subject;
    stringlower (subject);
```

```
        if ((strcmp (subject, "portrait") == 0) || (strcmp (subject, "landscape") == 0)
                || (strcmp (subject, "still-life") == 0) || (strcmp (subject, "other") == 0))
            valid = TRUE;
        else
        {
            cout << endl << "Invalid response!" << endl;
            cout << "Please enter one of the following:";
            cout << " portrait, landscape, still-life, other" << endl << endl;
        }
    }

} // Painting_Class::get_description

//-----------------------------------------------------------------------------------------

void Gallery_Class::get_gallery_information (void)
//
// retrieves gallery painting information
//
{
    cout << endl << endl;

    strcpy (purchase_date, current_date);

    cout << "Enter the NAME of the seller: ";
    cin >> seller_name;

    cout << "Enter the ADDRESS of the seller: ";
    cin >> seller_addr;

    cout << "Enter the purchase PRICE of the painting: ";
    cin >> purchase_price;

    target_price = purchase_price * TARGET_MARKUP;

} // Gallery_Class::get_gallery_information

//-----------------------------------------------------------------------------------------

void Gallery_Class::add_new_painting (void)
//
// inserts a gallery object in the proper place
//
{
    ifstream            in_file;        // stream object used for file input
    ofstream            out_file;       // stream object used for file output
    int                 found;          // indicates if object insertion point found
    Gallery_Class       temp_gallery;   // temporary object used for file copying

    found = FALSE;

    in_file.open ("gallery.dat", ios::in);

    if (in_file)
    {
```

136

```
            out_file.open ("temp_g.dat", ios::out);
            //
            // copy the current gallery file to a temporary file
            //
            while (!in_file.eof ())
            {
                //
                // read the temporary gallery object from the gallery file
                //
                temp_gallery.read_bought (in_file);

                //
                // write the temporary gallery object to a temporary file
                //
//++++++++++++++++++++++++++++++++++++++++++++++++++++++++++++++++++++++++
//
// additional code needed for compilation with Turbo C++ for Windows,
// but which need not be removed when other compilers are used
//
                if (strlen (temp_gallery.classification) != 0)
                    temp_gallery.write_bought (out_file);
//
//++++++++++++++++++++++++++++++++++++++++++++++++++++++++++++++++++++++++
            }

            in_file.close ();
            out_file.close ();

        } // if (in_file)

        out_file.open ("gallery.dat", ios::out);
        in_file.open ("temp_g.dat", ios::in);

        if (in_file)
        {
            //
            // copy the temporary file to new gallery file
            // while inserting the gallery object in the proper location
            //
            while (!in_file.eof ())
            {
                //
                // read a temporary gallery object from the temporary file
                //
                temp_gallery.read_bought (in_file);

//++++++++++++++++++++++++++++++++++++++++++++++++++++++++++++++++++++++++
//
// additional code needed for compilation with Turbo C++ for Windows,
// but which need not be removed when other compilers are used
//
                if (strlen (temp_gallery.classification) != 0)
//
//++++++++++++++++++++++++++++++++++++++++++++++++++++++++++++++++++++++++
                {
```

```
              //
              // write the proper object to the gallery file
              //
              if ((strcmp (temp_gallery.classification, classification)        <= 0) &&
                  (date_compare (temp_gallery.purchase_date, purchase_date) <= 0) &&
                  !found)
              {
                  //
                  // write the gallery object to the gallery file
                  //
                  write_bought (out_file);

                  //
                  // write the temporary gallery object to the gallery file
                  //
                  temp_gallery.write_bought (out_file);

                  found = TRUE;

              }
              else
                  temp_gallery.write_bought (out_file);
          }

      } // while (!in_file.eof ())

  } // if (in_file)

  //
  // write the gallery object to the end of the gallery file
  //
  if (!found)
      write_bought (out_file);

  in_file.close ();
  out_file.close ();

} // Gallery_Class::add_new_painting

//-------------------------------------------------------------------------------------------

void Gallery_Class::buy (void)
//
// allows user to buy a painting
//
{
    ifstream            in_file;            // stream object used for file input
    char                ch;                 // holds user response to Y/N question
    int                 found;              // indicates if painting already in gallery
    Gallery_Class       temp_gallery;       // temporary object used for file reading

    get_description ();

    found = FALSE;

    in_file.open ("gallery.dat", ios::in);
```

138

```
if (in_file)
{
    //
    // determine if the gallery object already exists in the gallery
    //
    while (!in_file.eof ())
    {
        //
        // read a temporary gallery object from the gallery file
        //
        temp_gallery.read_bought (in_file);
//++++++++++++++++++++++++++++++++++++++++++++++++++++++++++++++++++++++++
//
// additional code needed for compilation with Turbo C++ for Windows,
// but which need not be removed when other compilers are used
//
        if (strlen (temp_gallery.classification) != 0)
//
//++++++++++++++++++++++++++++++++++++++++++++++++++++++++++++++++++++++++
        {
            //
            // check if there is a match with the gallery object
            //
            if ((compare_str (temp_gallery.first_name, first_name) == 0) &&
                (compare_str (temp_gallery.last_name, last_name)  == 0) &&
                (compare_str (temp_gallery.title, title)          == 0))
            {
                found = TRUE;
                break;
            }

        } // if (strlen (temp_gallery.classification) != 0)

    } // while (!in_file.eof ())

    in_file.close ();

} // if (in_file)

if (found == TRUE)
{
    cout << endl << endl;
    cout << "The painting you described has already been purchased!\n\n";

}
else
{
    determine_alg_price ();

    cout << endl << endl;

    if (alg_price > 0)
    {
        cout << "The algorithm has determined the maximum offering price to be:\n";
        cout << "$" << alg_price << " million dollars.\n\n";
```

```
                    cout << "Do you want to purchase this painting (Y/N)? ";
                    fflush (stdin);
//+++++++++++++++++++++++++++++++++++++++++++++++++++++++++++++++++++++++
//
// additional code needed for compilation with the Sun C++ compiler,
// but which need not be removed when other compilers are used
//
//
                    cout << endl;
//
//+++++++++++++++++++++++++++++++++++++++++++++++++++++++++++++++++++++++

                    ch = getchar ();

                    if ((ch == 'Y') || (ch == 'y'))
                    {
                        get_gallery_information ();
                        add_new_painting ();
                    }
                }
            else
                    cout << "The algorithm has suggested that you should not buy this painting.";
        }

        cout << endl << endl;
        cout << " Press <ENTER> to return to main menu...";
        press_enter ();

} // Gallery_Class::buy

//-------------------------------------------------------------------------------------------

void Gallery_Class::bought_report (void)
//
// displays a report of bought paintings
//
{
        ifstream              in_file;            // stream object used for file input
        DATE_TYPE             one_less;           // date one year ago today
        int                   i;                  // counts number of paintings in report
        float                 total_purchase;     // sum of actual purchase prices
        float                 total_max;          // sum of maximum purchase prices

        total_purchase = 0.0;
        total_max = 0.0;
        i = 0;

        clear_screen ();
        subtract_one_year (current_date, one_less);

        in_file.open ("gallery.dat", ios::in);

        if (in_file)
        {
```

140

```
        //
        // read in all paintings from the gallery and
        // determine if they are candidates for the bought report
        //
        while (!in_file.eof ())
        {
            //
            // read a gallery object from the gallery file
            //
            read_bought (in_file);

//++++++++++++++++++++++++++++++++++++++++++++++++++++++++++++++++++++++++++++
//
// additional code needed for compilation with Turbo C++ for Windows,
// but which need not be removed when other compilers are used
//
//
            if (strlen (classification) != 0)
//
//++++++++++++++++++++++++++++++++++++++++++++++++++++++++++++++++++++++++++++
            {
                //
                // check if the painting was purchased within the past year
                //
                if (date_compare (one_less, purchase_date) <= 0)
                {
                    //
                    // pause the screen after every three paintings
                    //
                    if (((i % 3) == 0) && (i != 0))
                    {
                        cout << endl << endl;
                        cout << " Press <ENTER> to view the next screen...";
                        press_enter ();
                    }

                    //
                    // display a header message after every third painting
                    //
                    if ((i % 3) == 0)
                    {
                        clear_screen ();
                        cout << endl << endl;
                        cout << "\t\t        Report Date:" << current_date << endl;
                        cout << "\t\t    Osbert Oglesby - Collector of Fine Art\n";
                        cout << "\t\t          BOUGHT PAINTINGS\n\n";
                    }

                    cout << "----------------------------------------------------------------------------\n";
                    cout << "CLASSIFICATION: ";

                    if (purchase_price > alg_price)
                        cout << "*";

                    cout << classification << "   ";
```

```
                    cout << "\tPURCHASE DATE: " << purchase_date << endl;
                    cout << "LAST NAME:              " << last_name;
                    cout << "\t\tTITLE:                         " << title << endl;
                    cout << "SUGG. PRICE:      " << alg_price;
                    cout << "\t\tPURCHASE PRICE: " << purchase_price << endl;

                    total_purchase = total_purchase + purchase_price;
                    total_max = total_max + alg_price;

                    i++;

                } // if (date_compare (one_less, purchase_date) <= 0)

            } // if (strlen (classification) != 0)

        } // while (!in_file.eof ())

        in_file.close ();

    } // if (in_file)

    if (total_max > 0)
    {
        cout << endl << endl;
        cout << "Average ratio: " << (total_purchase / total_max);

    }
    else
        cout << "There have been no paintings bought within the past year.";

    cout << endl << endl;
    cout << " Press <ENTER> to return to main menu...";
    press_enter ();

} // Gallery_Class::bought_report

//-------------------------------------------------------------------------------------------------

void Gallery_Class::read_bought (ifstream& file_name)
                                    // stream object where gallery information is read
//
// reads a gallery object from file_name
//
{
    file_name >> classification >> first_name >> last_name;
    file_name >> title >> painting_date >> purchase_date;
    file_name >> medium >> subject >> seller_name >> seller_addr;
    file_name >> alg_price >> purchase_price >> target_price;
    file_name >> height >> width;

} // Gallery_Class::read_bought

//-------------------------------------------------------------------------------------------------

void Gallery_Class::write_bought (ofstream& file_name)
                                    // stream object where gallery information is written
```

```
//
// writes a gallery object to file_name
//
{
    file_name << classification << " " << first_name << " " << last_name << endl;
    file_name << title << " " << painting_date << " " << purchase_date << endl;
    file_name << medium << " " << subject << " " << seller_name << " " << seller_addr
            << endl;
    file_name << alg_price << " " << purchase_price << " " << target_price << endl;
    file_name << height << " " << width << endl;

} // Gallery_Class::write_bought
```

//---------------------------------------------------------------------------

```
void Gallery_Class::add_new_sale (void)
//
// records that a gallery painting has been sold
//
{
    ifstream                in_file;            // stream object used for file input
    ofstream                out_file;           // stream object used for file output
    int                     found;              // indicates if object insertion point found
    Gallery_Class           temp_gallery;       // temporary object used for file copying

    found = FALSE;

    in_file.open ("sold.dat", ios::in);

    if (in_file)
    {
        out_file.open ("temp_s.dat", ios::out);

        //
        // copy the current sold file to a temporary file
        //
        while (!in_file.eof ())
        {
            //
            // read a temporary gallery object from the sold file
            //
            temp_gallery.read_sold (in_file);

            //
            // write the temporary gallery object to the temporary file
            //
```
//++++++++++++++++++++++++++++++++++++++++++++++++++++++++++++++++++++++++++++
//
// additional code needed for compilation with Turbo C++ for Windows,
// but which need not be removed when other compilers are used
//
```
                if (strlen (temp_gallery.classification) != 0)
                    temp_gallery.write_sold (out_file);
```
//
//++++++++++++++++++++++++++++++++++++++++++++++++++++++++++++++++++++++++++++

```
        } // while (!in_file.eof ())

        in_file.close ();
        out_file.close ();
    } // if (in_file)

    out_file.open ("sold.dat", ios::out);
    in_file.open ("temp_s.dat", ios::in);

    if (in_file)
    {
        //
        // copy the temporary file to a new sold file
        // while inserting the painting object in the proper location
        //
        while (!in_file.eof ())
        {
            //
            // read a temporary gallery object from the temporary file
            //
            temp_gallery.read_sold (in_file);

//++++++++++++++++++++++++++++++++++++++++++++++++++++++++++++++++++++
//
// additional code needed for compilation with Turbo C++ for Windows,
// but which need not be removed when other compilers are used
//
            if (strlen (temp_gallery.classification) != 0)
//
//++++++++++++++++++++++++++++++++++++++++++++++++++++++++++++++++++++
            {
                //
                // write the proper object to the sold file
                //
                    if ((strcmp (temp_gallery.classification, classification)   <= 0) &&
                        (date_compare (temp_gallery.sale_date, sale_date)  <= 0) &&
                        !found)
                    {
                        //
                        // write the gallery object to the sold file
                        //
                        write_sold (out_file);

                        //
                        // write the temporary gallery object to the sold file
                        //
                        temp_gallery.write_sold (out_file);

                        found = TRUE;
                    }
                    else
                        temp_gallery.write_sold (out_file);

            } // if (strlen (temp_gallery.classification) != 0)
```

```
            } // while (!in_file.eof ())

      } // if (in_file)

      //
      // write the gallery object to the end of the sold file
      //
      if (!found)
          write_sold (out_file);

      in_file.close ();
      out_file.close ();

} // Gallery_Class::add_new_sale

//---------------------------------------------------------------------------------------------

void Gallery_Class::sell (void)
//
// allows user to sell a painting found in the gallery
//
{
      ifstream              in_file;              // stream object used for file input
      int                   found;                // indicates if painting already in gallery
      int                   already_sold;         // indicates if painting already sold
      NAME_TYPE             temp_fn;              // temp_fn, temp_ln, and temp_title
      NAME_TYPE             temp_ln;              // store temporary information about
      TITLE_TYPE            temp_title;           // the painting to be sold, namely
                                                  // first name, last name, and title, resp.

      clear_screen ();

      //
      // retrieve information about the painting desired to be sold
      //

      cout << endl << endl;
      cout << "Please enter the following information describing the painting:\n\n";
      cout << "Note: - Use an underscore in place of any spaces.\n";
      cout << "      - Do not leave any request blank.\n\n\n";

      cout << "Enter the FIRST name of the artist (append ? if uncertain): ";
      cin >> temp_fn;

      cout << "Enter the LAST name of the artist (append ? if uncertain): ";
      cin >> temp_ln;

      cout << "Enter the TITLE of the painting (append ? if uncertain): ";
      cin >> temp_title;

      already_sold = FALSE;

      in_file.open ("sold.dat", ios::in);

      if (in_file)
      {
```

```
        //
        // determine if the desired painting has already been sold
        //
        while (!in_file.eof ())
        {
            //
            // read a gallery object from the sold file
            //
            read_sold (in_file);

//++++++++++++++++++++++++++++++++++++++++++++++++++++++++++++++++++
//
// additional code needed for compilation with Turbo C++ for Windows,
// but which need not be removed when other compilers are used
//
            if (strlen (classification) != 0)
//
//++++++++++++++++++++++++++++++++++++++++++++++++++++++++++++++++++
            {
                //
                // check if there is a match with the gallery object
                //
                if ((compare_str (first_name, temp_fn) == 0) &&
                    (compare_str (last_name, temp_ln)  == 0) &&
                    (compare_str (title, temp_title)         == 0))
                {
                    already_sold = TRUE;
                    break;
                }
            } // if (strlen (classification) != 0)

        } // while (!in_file.eof ())

        in_file.close ();

    } // if (in_file)

    if (already_sold == TRUE)
    {
        cout << endl << endl;
        cout << "The painting you described has already been sold!\n\n";
    }
    else
    {
        found = FALSE;

        in_file.open ("gallery.dat", ios::in);

        if (in_file)
        {
            //
            // check to make sure that the desired painting
            // actually exists in the gallery
            //
            while (!in_file.eof ())
            {
```

146

```
                    //
                    // read a gallery object from the gallery file
                    //
                    read_bought (in_file);

//++++++++++++++++++++++++++++++++++++++++++++++++++++++++++++++++++++++
//
// additional code needed for compilation with Turbo C++ for Windows,
// but which need not be removed when other compilers are used
//
                    if (strlen (classification) != 0)
//
//++++++++++++++++++++++++++++++++++++++++++++++++++++++++++++++++++++++
                {
                        //
                        // check if there is a match with the desired painting
                        //
                        if ((compare_str (first_name, temp_fn) == 0) &&
                            (compare_str (last_name, temp_ln) == 0) &&
                            (compare_str (title, temp_title)    == 0))
                        {
                            found = TRUE;
                            break;
                        }

                } // if (strlen (classification) != 0)

            } // while (!in_file.eof ())

            in_file.close ();

        } // if (in_file)

        if (found == TRUE)
        {
            cout << endl << endl;
            cout << "Please enter the following sale information:\n\n\n";

            strcpy (sale_date, current_date);

            cout << "Enter the NAME of the buyer: ";
            cin >> buyer_name;

            cout << "Enter the ADDRESS of the buyer: ";
            cin >> buyer_addr;

            cout << "Enter the selling PRICE: ";
            cin >> sell_price;

            add_new_sale ();
            add_artist (first_name, last_name);

            cout << endl << endl;
            cout << "The sale has been recorded.";
        }
        else
```

```
                {
                        cout << endl << endl;
                        cout << "The painting you described can not be found in the gallery.\n";
                        cout << "Please make sure you entered the information correctly.\n";
                        cout << "Proper case is required.\n";
                }
        } // else (already_sold != TRUE)

        cout << endl << endl;
        cout << " Press <ENTER> to return to main menu...";
        press_enter ();

} // Gallery_Class::sell
```

//-------------------------------------------------------------------------------------------

```
void Gallery_Class::sell_report (void)
//
// displays a report of sold paintings
//
{
        ifstream              in_file;              // stream object used for file input
        DATE_TYPE             one_less;             // date one year ago today
        int                   i;                    // counts number of paintings in report
        float                 total_selling;        // sum of actual selling prices
        float                 total_target;         // sum of target prices

        total_selling = 0.0;
        total_target  = 0.0;
        i = 0;

        clear_screen ();
        subtract_one_year (current_date, one_less);

        in_file.open ("sold.dat", ios::in);

        if (in_file)
        {
                //
                // read in all paintings from the gallery and
                // determine if they are candidates for the sold report
                //
                while (!in_file.eof ())
                {
                        //
                        // read a gallery object from the sold file
                        //
                        read_sold (in_file);
```

//++++++++++++++++++++++++++++++++++++++++++++++++++++++++++++++++++++++++
```
//
// additional code needed for compilation with Turbo C++ for Windows,
// but which need not be removed when other compilers are used
//
                        if (strlen (classification) != 0)
```

148

```
//
//+++++++++++++++++++++++++++++++++++++++++++++++++++++++++++++++++++++++++

        {
            //
            // check if the painting was sold within the past year
            //
            if (date_compare (one_less, sale_date) <= 0)
            {
                //
                // pause the screen after every three paintings
                //
                if (((i % 3) == 0) && (i != 0))
                {
                    cout << endl << endl;
                    cout << " Press <ENTER> to view the next screen...";
                    press_enter ();

                }

                //
                // display a header message after every third painting
                //
                if ((i % 3) == 0)
                {
                    clear_screen ();
                    cout << endl << endl;
                    cout << "\t\t          Report Date:" << current_date << endl;
                    cout << "\t\t   Osbert Oglesby - Collector of Fine Art\n";
                    cout << "\t\t             SOLD PAINTINGS\n\n";
                }

                cout << "-----------------------------------------------------------------------------\n";
                cout << "CLASSIFICATION: ";

                if (sell_price < (target_price * 0.95))
                    cout << "*";

                cout << classification << "   ";
                cout << "\tSALE DATE:  " << sale_date << endl;
                cout << "LAST NAME:      " << last_name;
                cout << "\t\tTITLE:      " << title << endl;
                cout << "TARGET PRICE:  " << target_price;
                cout << "\t\tSELLING PRICE: " << sell_price << endl;

                total_selling = total_selling + sell_price;
                total_target = total_target + target_price;

                i++;

            } // if (date_compare (one_less, sale_date) <= 0)

        } // if (strlen (classification) != 0)

    } // while (!in_file.eof ())

    in_file.close ();
```

```
        } // if (in_file)

        cout << endl << endl;

        if (total_target > 0)
            cout << "Average ratio: " << (total_selling / total_target);
        else
            cout << "There have been no paintings sold within the past year.";

        cout << endl << endl;
        cout << " Press <ENTER> to return to main menu...";
        press_enter ();

} // Gallery_Class::sell_report

//---------------------------------------------------------------------------------------

void Gallery_Class::read_sold (ifstream& file_name)
                            // stream object where gallery information is read
//
// reads a sold gallery object from file_name
//
{
        file_name >> classification >> first_name >> last_name;
        file_name >> title >> painting_date >> purchase_date >> sale_date;
        file_name >> medium >> subject >> seller_name >> buyer_name;
        file_name >> seller_addr >> buyer_addr;
        file_name >> alg_price >> purchase_price >> target_price;
        file_name >> sell_price >> height >> width;

} // Gallery_Class::read_sold

//---------------------------------------------------------------------------------------

void Gallery_Class::write_sold (ofstream& file_name)
                            // stream object where gallery information is written
//
// writes a sold gallery object to file_name
//
{
        file_name << classification << " " << first_name << " " << last_name << endl;
        file_name << title << " " << painting_date << " " << purchase_date << " " << sale_date
                << endl;
        file_name << medium << " " << subject << " " << seller_name << " " << buyer_name
                << endl;
        file_name << seller_addr << " " << buyer_addr << endl;
        file_name << alg_price << " " << purchase_price << " " << target_price << endl;
        file_name << sell_price << " " << height << " " << width << endl;

} // Gallery_Class::write_sold

//---------------------------------------------------------------------------------------

void Gallery_Class::fashion_report (void)
//
```

```
// displays a report of fashionable painters and their paintings
//
{
    ifstream              art_file;              // stream object used for file input
    ifstream              sold_file;             // stream object used for file input
    DATE_TYPE             one_less;              // date one year ago today
    int                   i;                     // counts number of paintings in report
    int                   found;                 // indicates if qualified artists were found
    NAME_TYPE             temp_fn;               // temp_fn and temp_ln
    NAME_TYPE             temp_ln;               // stores values read from artist file,
                                                 // namely first name and last name, resp.

    i = 0;
    found = FALSE;

    clear_screen ();
    subtract_one_year (current_date, one_less);

    art_file.open ("artist.dat", ios::in);

    if (art_file)
    {
        //
        // read in all paintings from the gallery and
        // determine if they are candidates for the fashion report
        //
        while (!art_file.eof ())
        {
            //
            // read an artist name from the artist file
            //
            art_file >> temp_fn >> temp_ln;

            //
            // check if all of their paintings have sold over the target price
            //
            if ((strlen (temp_fn) != 0) && (over_target (temp_fn, temp_ln) == 0))
            {
                found = TRUE;
                clear_screen ();
                cout << endl << endl;
                cout << "\t\t          Report Date:" << current_date << endl;
                cout << "\t\t   Osbert Oglesby - Collector of Fine Art\n";
                cout << "\t\t             FASHION TRENDS\n\n";

                cout << "Painter: " << temp_fn << " " << temp_ln << endl;

                sold_file.open ("sold.dat", ios::in);

                //
                // examine every sold painting of the current artist
                // indicated by temp_fn, temp_ln
                //
                while (!sold_file.eof ())
                {
```

```
                    //
                    // read a painting object from the sold file
                    //
                    read_sold (sold_file);

//+++++++++++++++++++++++++++++++++++++++++++++++++++++++++++++++++++++++++++
//
// additional code needed for compilation with Turbo C++ for Windows,
// but which need not be removed when other compilers are used
//
                    if (strlen (classification) != 0)
//
//+++++++++++++++++++++++++++++++++++++++++++++++++++++++++++++++++++++++++++
                    {
                        //
                        // check if the painting was sold within the past year
                        // and make sure it was painted by the current artist
                        //
                        if ((date_compare (one_less, sale_date) <= 0) &&
                            (compare_str (temp_fn, first_name)   == 0) &&
                            (compare_str (temp_ln, last_name)    == 0))
                        {
                            //
                            // pause the screen after every three paintings
                            //
                            if (((i % 3) == 0) && (i != 0))
                            {
                                cout << endl << endl;
                                cout << " Press <ENTER> to view the next screen...";
                                press_enter ();

                                clear_screen ();
                                cout << endl << endl;
                                cout << "\t\t\t        Report Date:" << current_date << endl;
                                cout << "\t\t\t Osbert Oglesby - Collector of Fine Art\n";
                                cout << "\t\t\t          FASHION TRENDS\n\n";

                                cout << "Painter: " << temp_fn << " " << temp_ln << endl;

                            }

                            cout << "------------------------------------------------------------------------\n";
                            cout << "CLASSIFICATION: ";

                            cout << classification << "   ";
                            cout << "\t\tTITLE: " << title << endl;
                            cout << "SALE DATE:        " << sale_date << endl;
                            cout << "TARGET PRICE:    " << target_price;
                            cout << "\t\tSELLING PRICE: " << sell_price << endl;

                            i++;

                        } // if ((date_compare (one_less, sale_date) <= 0) &&

                    } // if (strlen (classification) != 0)
```

```
                    } // while (!sold_file.eof ())

                    cout << endl << endl;
                    cout << " Press <ENTER> to continue...";
                    press_enter ();

                    i = 0;
                    sold_file.close ();

                } // if ((strlen (temp_fn) != 0) && (over_target (temp_fn, temp_ln) == 0))

            } // while (!art_file.eof ())

            art_file.close ();

        } // if (art_file)

        if (!found)
            cout << "There are no artists who qualify for this report...";

        cout << endl << endl;
        cout << " Press <ENTER> to return to main menu...";
        press_enter ();

} // Gallery_Class::fashion_report

//------------------------------------------------------------------------------------

void Auction_Class::read_auction (ifstream& file_name)
                                // stream object where auction information is read
//
// reads an auction object from file_name
//
{
    file_name >> first_name >> last_name >> title >> painting_date;
    file_name >> height >> width >> medium;
    file_name >> subject >> auction_date >> auction_price;

} // Auction_Class::read_auction

//------------------------------------------------------------------------------------

void Masterpiece_Class::determine_alg_price (void)
//
// determines the maximum price to be offered for a masterpiece
//
{
    ifstream        in_file;        // stream object used for file input
    float           high;           // keeps track of highest similarity
    float           alg_high;       // price of most similar work
    float           temp;           // number of matches on medium/subject
    float           auction_area;   // area of an auction painting
    float           gallery_area;   // area of a gallery painting
    int             i;              // loop iterator for compound interest
    int             auction_year;   // year of auction painting sale date
```

```
int                    current_year;     // year component of current_date
int                    month;            // dummy variable for call to breakup_date
int                    day;              // dummy variable for call to breakup_date
DATE_TYPE              high_date;        // date of most similar work
Auction_Class          temp_auction;     // temporary object used for file reading

high = 0.0;
alg_high = 0.0;

strcpy (high_date, current_date);

in_file.open ("auction.dat", ios::in);

if (in_file)
{
    //
    // loop through all of the auction objects and find the most similar work
    //
    while (!in_file.eof ())
    {
        //
        // read an auction object
        //
        temp_auction.read_auction (in_file);

//+++++++++++++++++++++++++++++++++++++++++++++++++++++++++++++++++++++++
//
// additional code needed for compilation with Turbo C++ for Windows,
// but which need not be removed when other compilers are used
//
        if (strlen (temp_auction.get_first_name ()) != 0)
//
//+++++++++++++++++++++++++++++++++++++++++++++++++++++++++++++++++++++++
        {
            temp = 0.0;

            //
            // if the artist names match, compute the similarity
            //
            if ((compare_str (temp_auction.get_first_name (), first_name) == 0) &&
                (compare_str (temp_auction.get_last_name (), last_name)   == 0))
            {
                if (strcmp (temp_auction.get_medium (), medium) == 0)
                    temp++;

                if (strcmp (temp_auction.get_subject (), subject) == 0)
                    temp++;

                auction_area = temp_auction.get_height () * temp_auction.get_width ();
                gallery_area  = height * width;

                if (auction_area > gallery_area)
                    temp = temp * gallery_area / auction_area;
                else
                    temp = temp * auction_area / gallery_area;
```

```
                                    //
                                    // a higher similarity was found...
                                    //
                                    if (temp > high)
                                    {
                                        high = temp;
                                        alg_high = temp_auction.get_auction_price ();
                                        strcpy (high_date, temp_auction.get_auction_date ());
                                    }

                        } // if ((compare_str (temp_auction.get_first_name (), first_name) == 0)

                    } // if (strlen (temp_auction.get_first_name ()) != 0)

                } // while (!in_file.eof ())

                in_file.close ();

        } // if (in_file)

        //
        // find the year components of the auction date and current date
        //
        breakup_date (high_date, auction_year, day, month);
        breakup_date (current_date, current_year, day, month);

        //
        // compute the compound interest
        //
        for (i = auction_year; i < current_year; i++)
            alg_high = alg_high * ANNUAL_INTEREST;

        alg_price = alg_high;

} // Masterpiece_Class::determine_alg_price

//-------------------------------------------------------------------------------------------------

void Masterwork_Class::determine_alg_price (void)
//
// determines the maximum price to be offered for a masterwork
//
{
    int                    century;                // century in which painting was created

        //
        // first, compute the price of the painting as if it were a masterpiece
        //
        Masterpiece_Class::determine_alg_price ();

        //
        // next, obtain the century in which the painting was created and adjust
        // the price based upon the century
        //
```

```
        century = atoi (painting_date) / 100;

        if (century == 19)
            alg_price = alg_price * 0.25;
        else
            alg_price = alg_price * (20 - century) / (21 - century);

} // Masterwork_Class::determine_alg_price

//-----------------------------------------------------------------------------------------------

void Other_Class::determine_alg_price (void)
//
// determines the maximum price to be offered for an "other" piece of work
//
{
        ifstream                in_file;                // stream object used for file input
        float                   fashion_coefficient;    // current coefficient of painting artist
        Fashionability_Class    temp_fash;              // temp. fashionability object
                                                        // used for file reading

        fashion_coefficient = 0.0;

        in_file.open ("fash.dat", ios::in);

        if (in_file)
        {
            //
            // loop through the fashionability file to find a match with the artist
            //
            while (!in_file.eof ())
            {
                //
                // read in an object from the fashionability file
                //
                temp_fash.read_fash (in_file);

//+++++++++++++++++++++++++++++++++++++++++++++++++++++++++++++++++++++++++++
//
// additional code needed for compilation with Turbo C++ for Windows,
// but which need not be removed when other compilers are used
//
                if (strlen (temp_fash.get_first_name ()) != 0)
//
//+++++++++++++++++++++++++++++++++++++++++++++++++++++++++++++++++++++++++++
                {
                    //
                    // check if there is a match with the current other object
                    //
                    if ((compare_str (temp_fash.get_first_name (), first_name) == 0) &&
                        (compare_str (temp_fash.get_last_name (), last_name)  == 0))
                    {
                        fashion_coefficient = temp_fash.get_coefficient ();
                        break;
                    }
```

```
        } // if (strlen (temp_fash.get_first_name ()) != 0)

     } // while (!in_file.eof ())

     in_file.close ();

  } // if (in_file)

  alg_price = fashion_coefficient * height * width;

} // Other_Class::determine_alg_price
```

//-------------------------------------------------------------------------------------------------

```
void Fashionability_Class::get_description (void)
//
// retrieves fashionability description information
//
{
   clear_screen ();

   //
   // request fashionability object information
   //

   cout << "Please enter the following information concerning the artist whose\n";
   cout << "fashionability coefficient you wish to change.\n\n";
   cout << "Note: - Use an underscore in place of any spaces.\n";
   cout << "      - Do not leave any request blank.\n\n\n";

   cout << "Enter the FIRST name of the artist: ";
   cin >> first_name;

   cout << "Enter the LAST name of the artist: ";
   cin >> last_name;

   cout << "Enter the new fashionability coefficient for this artist: ";
   cin >> coefficient;

} // Fashionability_Class::get_description
```

//-------------------------------------------------------------------------------------------------

```
void Fashionability_Class::read_fash (ifstream& file_name)
                                    // stream object where fashionability information is read
//
// reads a fashionability object from file_name
//
{
   file_name >> first_name >> last_name >> coefficient;

} // Fashionability_Class::read_fash
```

//-------------------------------------------------------------------------------------------------

```
void Fashionability_Class::write_fash (ofstream& file_name)
                           // stream object where fashionability information is written
//
// writes a fashionability object to file_name
//
{
    file_name << first_name << " " << last_name << " " << coefficient << endl;

} // Fashionability_Class::write_fash

//-------------------------------------------------------------------------------------------

void Fashionability_Class::add_new_fash (void)
//
// allows the user to add/update the fashionability coefficient
// of an object of Fashionability_Class
//
{
    ifstream              in_file;        // stream object used for file input
    ofstream              out_file;       // stream object used for file output
    int                   found;          // indicates if object insertion point found
    Fashionability_Class  temp_fash;      // temporary object used for file copying

    //
    // obtain information about the new fashionability object
    //
    get_description ();

    found = FALSE;

    in_file.open ("fash.dat", ios::in);

    if (in_file)
    {
        out_file.open ("temp_f.dat", ios::out);

        //
        // copy the current fashionability file to a temporary file
        //
        while (!in_file.eof ())
        {
            //
            // read a temporary object from the fashionability file
            //
            temp_fash.read_fash (in_file);

            //
            // write the temporary fashionability object to the temporary file
            //
//++++++++++++++++++++++++++++++++++++++++++++++++++++++++++++++++++++++++
//
// additional code needed for compilation with Turbo C++ for Windows,
// but which need not be removed when other compilers are used
//
            if (strlen (temp_fash.first_name) != 0)
```

```
                    temp_fash.write_fash (out_file);
//
//++++++++++++++++++++++++++++++++++++++++++++++++++++++++++++++++++++++++
        }

        out_file.close ();
        in_file.close ();

    } // if (in_file)

    out_file.open ("fash.dat", ios::out);
    in_file.open ("temp_f.dat", ios::in);

    if (in_file)
    {
        //
        // copy the temporary file to a new fashionability file
        // while updating/inserting the fashionability object
        //
        while (!in_file.eof ())
        {
            //
            // read a temporary fashionability object from the temporary file
            //
            temp_fash.read_fash (in_file);

//++++++++++++++++++++++++++++++++++++++++++++++++++++++++++++++++++++++++
//
// additional code needed for compilation with Turbo C++ for Windows,
// but which need not be removed when other compilers are used
//
            if (strlen (temp_fash.first_name) != 0)
//
//++++++++++++++++++++++++++++++++++++++++++++++++++++++++++++++++++++++++
            {
                //
                // write the proper object to the fashionability file
                //
                if ((compare_str (temp_fash.first_name, first_name) == 0) &&
                    (compare_str (temp_fash.last_name, last_name)  == 0))
                {
                    write_fash (out_file);
                    found = TRUE;
                }
                else
                    temp_fash.write_fash (out_file);
            } // if (strlen (temp_fash.first_name) != 0)

        } // while (!in_file.eof ())

        in_file.close ();

    } // if (in_file)

    //
```

```
// write the fashionability object to the end of the fashionability file
//
if (!found)
    write_fash (out_file);

out_file.close ();

cout << endl << endl;
cout << " Press <ENTER> to return to main menu...";
press_enter ();

} // Fashionability_Class::add_new_fash
```

//------------------------------------------------------------------------------------------------

```
void main (void)
{
    int                    date_ok;           // indicates if current date properly entered

    date_ok = FALSE;

    //
    // initialize float output to two digits after the decimal point
    //
    cout.precision (2);
    cout.setf (ios::showpoint);
    cout.setf (ios::fixed);

    while (!date_ok)
    {
        cout << "Please enter today's date (mm/dd/yy): ";
        cin >> current_date;

        if (valid_date (current_date) == 0)
            date_ok = TRUE;
        else
        {
            cout << "You entered the date incorrectly.\n";
            cout << "Please use the format mm/dd/yy.\n";
        }
    }

    display_main_menu ();

} // main
```

//------------------------------------------------------------------------------------------------

```
void add_artist (char *fn,                    // first name of artist to be added
                 char *ln)                    // last name of artist to be added
//
// inserts an artist name into the artist file
//
{
    ifstream               in_file;           // stream object used for file input
    ofstream               out_file;          // stream object used for file output
```

160

```
NAME_TYPE              temp_fn;          // temporary string used for file copying
NAME_TYPE              temp_ln;          // temporary string used for file copying
int                    found;            // indicates if artist insertion point found

found = FALSE;

in_file.open ("artist.dat", ios::in);

if (in_file)
{
    out_file.open ("temp_art.dat", ios::out);

    //
    // the following loop copies the current artist file to a temporary file
    //
    while (!in_file.eof ())
    {
        //
        // read a temporary name from the artist file
        //
        in_file >> temp_fn >> temp_ln;

        //
        // write the temporary name to the temporary file
        //
//+++++++++++++++++++++++++++++++++++++++++++++++++++++++++++++++++++++++++++
//
// additional code needed for compilation with Turbo C++ for Windows,
// but which need not be removed when other compilers are used
//
        if (strlen (temp_fn) != 0)
            out_file << temp_fn << " " << temp_ln << endl;
//
//+++++++++++++++++++++++++++++++++++++++++++++++++++++++++++++++++++++++++++
    }

    out_file.close ();
    in_file.close ();

} // if (in_file)

out_file.open ("artist.dat", ios::out);
in_file.open ("temp_art.dat", ios::in);

if (in_file)
{
    //
    // copy the temporary file to a new artist file
    // while inserting the new artist name in the proper location
    //
    while (!in_file.eof ())
    {
        //
        // read a temporary name from the temporary file
        //
```

```
            in_file >> temp_fn >> temp_ln;

//+++++++++++++++++++++++++++++++++++++++++++++++++++++++++++++++++++++
//
// additional code needed for compilation with Turbo C++ for Windows,
// but which need not be removed when other compilers are used
//
            if (strlen (temp_fn) != 0)
//
//+++++++++++++++++++++++++++++++++++++++++++++++++++++++++++++++++++++
            {
                //
                // write the proper record to the artist file in alphabetical order
                //
                if ((compare_str (temp_ln, ln) < 0) || (found == TRUE))
                    out_file << temp_fn << " " << temp_ln << endl;
                else
                {
                    if (compare_str (temp_ln, ln) > 0)
                    {
                        out_file << fn << " " << ln << endl;
                        found = TRUE;
                    }
                    else
                    {
                        if (compare_str (temp_fn, fn) < 0)
                            out_file << temp_fn << " " << temp_ln << endl;
                        else
                        {
                            out_file << fn << " " << ln << endl;
                            found = TRUE;
                        }
                    }
                }
            } // if (strlen (temp_fn) != 0)

        } // while (!in_file.eof ())

        in_file.close ();

    } // if (in_file)

    //
    // write the artist name to the end of the artist file
    //
    if (!found)
        out_file << fn << " " << ln << endl;

    out_file.close ();

} // add_artist

//------------------------------------------------------------------------------------

int over_target(char *fn,              // first name of artist under examination
                char *ln)              // last name of artist under examination
```

162

```
//
// examines all the sold paintings and determines if the artist represented
//  by the string parameters fn and ln (first name/last name) has had all of his or her
// paintings sold over the target price during the past year (with at least 2 sales).
// Returns 0 if all paintings were sold over the target price,
// returns -1 otherwise
//
{
        ifstream              in_file;           // stream object used for file input
        DATE_TYPE             one_less;          // date one year ago today
        int                   count;             // # of paintings sold over target price
        int                   found;             // denotes if all paintings sold over target
        Gallery_Class         temp_gallery;      // temporary object used for file reading

        count = 0;
        found = TRUE;

        subtract_one_year (current_date, one_less);

        in_file.open ("sold.dat", ios::in);

        if (in_file)
        {

            //
            // examine all of the paintings that have been sold
            //
            while (!in_file.eof ())
            {
                //
                // read a temporary gallery object from the sold file
                //
                temp_gallery.read_sold (in_file);

//++++++++++++++++++++++++++++++++++++++++++++++++++++++++++++++++++++++++
//
// additional code needed for compilation with Turbo C++ for Windows,
// but which need not be removed when other compilers are used
//
                if (strlen (temp_gallery.get_classification ()) != 0)
//
//++++++++++++++++++++++++++++++++++++++++++++++++++++++++++++++++++++++++
                {
                    //
                    // ensure that the temporary gallery object is the desired artist
                    // and that the sale happened within the past year
                    //
                    if ((date_compare (one_less, temp_gallery.get_sale_date ()) <= 0) &&
                        (compare_str (fn, temp_gallery.get_first_name ())    == 0) &&
                        (compare_str (ln, temp_gallery.get_last_name ())     == 0))

                    {
                        if (temp_gallery.get_sell_price () > temp_gallery.get_target_price ())
                            count++;
```

```
                    else
                        found = FALSE;
                }

            } // if (strlen (temp_gallery.get_classification ()) != 0)

        } // while (!in_file.eof ())

    } // if (in_file)

    in_file.close ();

    //
    // return 0 iff all paintings sold in the past year were over the target
    // price (found == TRUE) and there were at least 2 sales (count > 1)
    //
    if (found == TRUE && count > 1)
        return 0;
    else
        return -1;

} // over_target

//---------------------------------------------------------------------------------

void clear_screen (void)
//
//
// clears the screen
//
{
    int                     i;                  // loop counter representing number of
                                                // blank lines to be printed

    //
    // implementation-dependent code to clear the screen should replace
    // the code given below
    //

    for (i = 0; i < 26; i++)
        cout << endl;

} // clear_screen

//---------------------------------------------------------------------------------

void press_enter (void)
//
// waits until the user presses the <ENTER> key
//
{

    char                    ch;                 // dummy variable used
                                                // to induce keyboard input
```

```
    fflush (stdin);
//+++++++++++++++++++++++++++++++++++++++++++++++++++++++++++++++++++++++
//
// additional code needed for compilation with the Sun C++ compiler,
// but which need not be removed when other compilers are used
//
//
    cout << endl;
//
//+++++++++++++++++++++++++++++++++++++++++++++++++++++++++++++++++++++++
    ch = getchar ();

} // press_enter

//---------------------------------------------------------------------------

void display_main_menu (void)
//
// displays the main menu containing all the options available to the user
//
{

    int                 done;           // terminates do-loop
    int                 choice;         // user's choice
    Gallery_Class       painting;       // painting object to be sold

    done = FALSE;
    while (!done)
    {
        clear_screen ();
        cout << "\t                    MAIN MENU\n\n\n";
        cout << "\t            Osbert Oglesby - Collector of Fine Art\n\n\n";
        cout << "\t                1. Buy a Painting\n\n";
        cout << "\t                2. Sell a Painting\n\n";
        cout << "\t                3. Produce a Report\n\n";
        cout << "\t                4. Quit\n\n\n";
        cout << "\t            Enter your choice and press <ENTER>: ";
        cin >> choice;

        switch (choice)
        {
            case 1:
                display_buy_painting_menu ();
                break;

            case 2:
                painting.sell ();
                break;

            case 3:
                display_report_menu ();
                break;

            case 4:
                done = TRUE;
                break;
```

165

```cpp
            default:
                cout << endl << endl << "Choice is out of range\n\n";
                cout << "     Press <ENTER> to return to menu...";
                press_enter ();
                break;

        } // switch (choice)

    } // while (!done)

} // display_main_menu

//-------------------------------------------------------------------------------------------------

void display_buy_painting_menu (void)
//
// allows user to select the type of painting to be purchased
//
{

    int                 done;           // terminates do-loop
    int                 choice;         // user's choice
    Masterpiece_Class   masterpiece;    // item to be bought
    Masterwork_Class    masterwork;     // item to be bought
    Other_Class         other;          // item to be bought
    Fashionability_Class fash;          // item to be updated

    done = FALSE;
    while (!done)
    {
        clear_screen ();
        cout << "              BUY PAINTING MENU\n\n\n";
        cout << "        Osbert Oglesby - Collector of Fine Art\n\n\n";
        cout << "\t      1. Buy a Masterpiece\n\n";
        cout << "\t      2. Buy a Masterwork\n\n";
        cout << "\t      3. Buy an Other piece of work\n\n";
        cout << "\t      4. Update Fashionability Coefficient\n\n";
        cout << "\t      5. Return to Main Menu\n\n\n";
        cout << "        Enter your choice and press <ENTER>: ";
        cin >> choice;

        switch (choice)
        {
            case 1:
                masterpiece.buy ();
                break;

            case 2:
                masterwork.buy ();
                break;

            case 3:
                other.buy ();
                break;
```

```
                case 4:
                    fash.add_new_fash ();
                    break;

                case 5:
                    done = TRUE;
                    break;

                default:
                    cout << endl << endl << "Choice is out of range\n\n";
                    cout << "    Press <ENTER> to return to menu...";
                    press_enter ();
                    break;

        } // switch (choice)

    } // while (!done)

} // display_buy_painting_menu

//-------------------------------------------------------------------------------------------------

void display_report_menu (void)
//
// allows user to select the type of report to be displayed
//
{

    int                 done;               // terminates do-loop
    int                 choice;             // user's choice
    Gallery_Class       painting;           // item used to invoke report

    done = FALSE;
    while (!done)
    {
        clear_screen ();
        cout << "                REPORT MENU\n\n\n";
        cout << "        Osbert Oglesby - Collector of Fine Art\n\n\n";
        cout << "            1. Report on Bought Paintings\n\n";
        cout << "            2. Report on Sold Paintings\n\n";
        cout << "            3. Report on Fashion Trends\n\n";
        cout << "            4. Return to Main Menu\n\n\n";
        cout << "        Enter your choice and press <ENTER>: ";
        cin >> choice;

        switch (choice)
        {
            case 1:
                painting.bought_report ();
                break;

            case 2:
                painting.sell_report ();
                break;

            case 3:
                painting.fashion_report ();
```

```
                break;

            case 4:
                done = TRUE;
                break;

            default:
                cout << endl << endl << "Choice is out of range\n\n";
                cout << "     Press <ENTER> to return to menu...";
                press_enter ();
                break;

        } // switch (choice)

    } // while (!done)

} // display_report_menu
```

//-------------------------------------------------------------------------------------------------

```
void breakup_date (char *date,          // string containing date to be partitioned
                   int &year,           // year component of date
                   int &month,          // month component of date
                   int &day)            // day component of date
//
// given a valid date in the format MM/DD/YY, returns the
// integer components of the respective year, month, and day
//
{
    char           temp[3];             // for storing parts of date

    temp[2] = '\0';

    //
    // retrieve the year component from the date string
    //
    temp[0] = date[6];
    temp[1] = date[7];
    year = atoi (temp);

    //
    // retrieve the day component from the date string
    //
    temp[0] = date[3];
    temp[1] = date[4];
    day = atoi (temp);

    //
    // retrieve the month component from the date string
    //
    temp[0]  = date[0];
    temp[1]  = date[1];
    month = atoi (temp);

} // breakup_date
```

```
//----------------------------------------------------------------------------------------------

int valid_date (char *date)        // string containing date to be verified
//
// determines if the string contained in date corresponds to a valid date
// of the form mm/dd/yy, where 1 <= mm <= 12, 1 <= dd <= 31, 0 <= yy <= 99
// return 0 iff the date is valid
//
{
    int                        year;            // year component of date
    int                        month;           // month component of date
    int                        day;             // day component of date

    //
    // ensure that the slashes are in the proper place
    //
    if ((date[2] != '/') || (date[5] != '/'))
        return -1;

    //
    // obtain all the integer components of date
    //
    breakup_date (date, year, month, day);

    //
    // check that the year component makes sense
    //
    if ((year < 0) || (year > 99))
        return -1;

    //
    // check that the month component makes sense
    //
    if ((month < 1) || (month > 12))
        return -1;

    //
    // check that the day component makes sense
    //
    if ((day < 1) || (day > 31))
        return -1;
    else
        return 0;

} // valid_date

//----------------------------------------------------------------------------------------------

int date_compare (char *date1,                 // string of the form mm/dd/yy
                  char *date2)                 // string of the form mm/dd/yy
// determines the temporal order of two dates
// returns -1 if date1 < date2
// returns 0 if the dates are the same
// returns 1 if date2 < date1
```

```
//
{
    int                     year1;              // year component of date1
    int                     year2;              // year component of date2
    int                     month1;             // month component of date1
    int                     month2;             // month component of date2
    int                     day1;               // day component of date1
    int                     day2;               // day component of date2

    breakup_date (date1, year1, month1, day1);
    breakup_date (date2, year2, month2, day2);

    //
    // first, compare the respective years
    //
    if (year1 < year2)
        return -1;

    if (year1 > year2)
        return 1;

    //
    // next, compare the months
    //
    if (month1 < month2)
        return -1;

    if (month1 > month2)
        return 1;

    //
    // finally, compare the respective days
    //
    if (day1 < day2)
        return -1;

    if (day1 > day2)
        return 1;
    else
        return 0;

} // date_compare

//------------------------------------------------------------------------------------------------

void subtract_one_year (char *date1,         // string of the form mm/dd/yy
                        char *date2)         // string of the form mm/dd/yy
// given the string in date1 (in the format mm/dd/yy), this function will
// construct date2 which represents mm/dd/(yy −1)
//
{
    int                     year;               // year component of a date
    int                     month;              // month component of a date
    int                     day;                // day component of a date
    char                    temp[3];            // for storing parts of a date
```

170

```
        temp[2] = '\0';

        //
        // initially, make date2 equal to date1
        //
        strcpy (date2, date1);

        //
        // obtain the integer components of date2
        //
        breakup_date (date2, year, month, day);

        //
        // decrement the year component and convert to a temporary string
        //
        year--;
        sprintf (temp, "%d", year);

        //
        // the following handles the case when the year is a single digit
        //
        if (year < 10)
        {
            temp[1] = temp[0];
            temp[0] = '0';
        }

        //
        // replace the year component with the temporary string
        //
        date2[6] = temp[0];
        date2[7] = temp[1];

} // subtract_one_year

//-------------------------------------------------------------------------------------------

void remove_q (char *s,              // a string which may contain
                                     // question marks
               char *t)              // a string void of any question marks
//
// copies the contents of string s into string t while removing any
// question marks
//
{
    int             i;               // iterates over the length of string s
    int             count;           // index counter for string t

    count = 0;

    for (i = 0; i <= strlen (s); i++)
        //
        // copy only the non-question mark characters
        //
```

```
        if (s[i] != '?')
        {
            t[count] = s[i];
            count++;
        }

} // remove_q

//------------------------------------------------------------------------------------

int compare_str (char *s, char *t)            // represents the two strings to compare
//
// compares two strings in the same manner as strcmp while ignoring any
// question marks
//
{
    char            temp_s[42];               // represents s void of any question marks
    char            temp_t[42];               // represents t void of any question marks

    //
    // remove all question marks from both strings
    //
    remove_q (s, temp_s);
    remove_q (t, temp_t);

    //
    // compare the two strings without question marks
    //
    return strcmp (temp_s, temp_t);

} // compare_str

//------------------------------------------------------------------------------------

void stringlower (char *s)                    // the string to convert to lowercase
//
// converts characters of string s to lowercase if needed
//
{
    int             i;                        // index counter for string s

    for (i = 0; i <= strlen (s); i++)
    //
    // change the current character to lowercase if needed
    //
    if (isupper(s[i]))
        s[i] = tolower(s[i]);

} // stringlower

//------------------------------------------------------------------------------------
```

# CHAPTER 14

## MAINTENANCE PHASE

I have found that this chapter is a good place to repeat the message regarding the importance of maintenance. I think that the case study of Section 14.3 is worth going into in some detail, because it illustrates so many aspects of maintenance. (Like the other anecdotes in *Classical and Object-Oriented Software Engineering*, this one is also perfectly true. I have disguised the country and the name of the organization to protect the innocent. Instructors who would like to know the real names are welcome to contact me.)

Section 14.7 covers reverse engineering. The topic is becoming increasingly important as more and more organizations are attempting to upgrade their software.

## PROBLEM SOLUTIONS

14.1: Maintenance usually involves changes to other people's work, so it is mistakenly viewed as a noncreative task. Also, since development of a complete product usually involves many more person-months than one single maintenance task, development tasks produce more revenue than maintenance tasks, and hence better professionals are put to work meeting the development deadlines to bring in the money. The flaw in this argument can be seen by measuring the total annual revenue from development and from maintenance.

14.2: Every computer can, in theory, be infected with viruses. Thus, certain modules will have multiple variations so that the product can be run on many different computers and operating systems.

Turning now to the individual viruses, it is true that a given virus will usually be specific to a certain hardware/operating system combination. However, there are those who will modify a virus so that it infects other hardware and/or operating systems. Thus many of the modules that check for the presence of a specific virus will also have to be able to be run on a wide variety of different computers and operating systems

14.3: There are different indexing schemes for books; there are also different bar code schemes. In addition, some libraries may not be able to afford bar-code scanners and will use keyboard input. There are different operating systems and different hardware on which the library system may be implemented. There are different types of libraries with different circulation policies. Also, some libraries are branches of an overall library system, all sharing the same books.

14.4: ATM hardware will vary from bank to bank, as will the hardware/operating system of the computer controlling the ATM network. Each bank will have different policies regarding the operations that may be performed at an ATM; for example, credit cards may not be supported, or only one credit card account. The maximum amount of money that can be withdrawn per day may vary. Also, if the ATM system is implemented in foreign countries, aspects of the product will have to be changed. Finally, not only banks use ATMs, but also a wide variety of other financial institutions.

14.5: There is an immense variety of personal computers/operating systems on which such a product could be implemented.

14.6: A broad range of software engineering skills (especially documentation) and superb diagnostic skills are needed. Good interpersonal skills are desirable, especially if he or she will be dealing with clients.

14.7: Because of the possibility that the organization will expand or be sold to someone else, one-person software maintenance should not be different in any way from maintenance by a larger organization.

14.8: Data stored in file: name of product; serial number of client's version; version configuration, including hardware, operating system and compiler details; date and time fault was detected; fault category (some sort of categorization scheme must be set up); details of any error messages reported by the product or operating system; name of person reporting the fault; textual description of the problem; repair status of fault, including recommended ways to work around it; previous reports that seem to be related to this fault; management information such as name of maintenance programmer, and time devoted to each change.

Queries that could be answered include: fault status; billing information for each product, configuration, version, client; reported fault rates by product, configuration, version, client, hardware, operating system, and/or fault category; correlations between these variables; which keywords occur frequently in textual descriptions.

Query that could not be answered: precisely how to fix the fault.

14.9: Configuration control tools and reverse engineering tools are probably the most important CASE tools needed to help maintain the existing COBOL code.

## TERM PROJECT

14.10: All dates should be represented in the format mm/dd/yyyy. It is likely that, in most implementations, only a small number of modules would be affected. More specifically, changes would be restricted to those parts of the code which perform operations on dates (e.g., a function which compares two dates, or checks whether a given date is valid). If the system was designed properly, then the methods which utilize these date operations are unlikely to need to be changed.

In addition, the formula for computing the maximum purchase price of a masterwork will need to be extended to masterworks painted in the twenty-first century.